Now I Know

Ella W. Taylor

Copyright © 2020 by Ella Taylor

All rights reserved. No part of this book may be reproduced, stored or transmitted in any form or by any means—mechanical, electronic, recording, photocopy or other means—without the written permission of the author.

Illustrations: Herby Augustin
Photograph on Page 17: Comfreak (pixbay.com)
Photograph on Page 61: Kymberly Rosenthal
Photograph on Page 79: Jill Wellington (Pixbay.com)
Cover Design: Marcelle Costanza

Publisher: PrintPOD Publishing
Hillsborough, New Jersey

Editor: Dina Forbes
Production Coordinator: Michael Aslett
Production Editor: Kymberly Rosenthal

Contact: printpodpub@gmail.com
Phone: 908-917-3400

Printed in the United States of America

First Edition 2020

ISBN: 978-0-578-66612-9

Dedication

To my deceased mother and father, Margaret and Earl Branch

First, I dedicate this book to my mother to express my gratitude for introducing me to the greatest, highest power there is: God. I'll never forget her method of teaching, which was by living her truth. I simply watched her all the time. She was a rare individual—undoubtedly the most remarkable uneducated person I have ever known.

I also dedicate this book to my father. He exemplified the three P's: he was *present*, he was a good *provider,* and he was a good *protector.* He was a very stern father with lots of rules, but I knew he loved me, and he made me believe I was a very special person. He made me feel like a princess. My father could barely read and write, but he would constantly drill into his children the importance of getting an education. Because of his passionate advocacy of education, I went to college for ten years at night while working full time and raising a family. It was like an addiction. I think that perhaps, even in death, I was simply afraid to disobey my father. Long after my father died, many times when I became discouraged with going to school, I would conjure up images of him preaching about the critical value of a college education. These images reinforced my appreciation for education, motivated me to complete my education, and ultimately elevated me to a high level of success in corporate America.

On reflection, I realized that my parents taught me to believe in God, believe in myself, and believe in the importance of education.

Table of Contents

Acknowledgments	11
Introduction	15
Part 1: My World Collapses	**17**
The Ever-Evolving Ella	19
Willie Disappears	22
Finding Willie	25
The Murder Scene	26
The Aftermath	29
The Funeral	35
Why the Murder?	47
Finding the Murderer	50
The Arraignment	54
The Appeal	57
Part 2: My Healing Journey	**61**
Taking the First Step	62
Life Without Willie	63
God Is in Control of Everything	63
A Newness in Me	64
God's Plan for My Life	65
Therapy	67
Living With the Family	72
My Best Friend	74

Part 3: My New Life ... 79

    Who Am I Now? ... 80

    Life Lessons ... 82

    My Angels ... 108

    What Is an Earth Angel? ... 109

    My Five Tips for Living a Better Life ... 111

    Putting It All Together ... 116

    About the Author ... 119

Acknowledgements

Writing this book has been quite a challenge. But fortunately, I've had excellent help. My primary thanks belong to my Lord and Savior, Jesus Christ, who directed me to the absolute best publication team this side of heaven. My team—defined as a group of people who work together for a common cause—consisted of Kym, Jackie, Mike, and Dina, all of whom have done a phenomenal job in guiding me through the entire process to publish my first book.

Thank you, Kym Rosenthal. God led me to you at Planet Fitness gym. In October 2018, for reasons that weren't clear to me at the time, I felt drawn to initiate a conversation with you after we finished an exercise class. During our talk, I asked you, "What do you do?" You replied, "I help instruct a class to teach people how to write books." All I could say was, "Oh my goodness! I've wanted to write a book for more than five years now, but I didn't know where to start." Well, the rest is history. I joined your class in November 2018 and finished writing my story in August 2019. You gave me the materials I needed to get started, provided me with helpful guidance, and introduced me to the rest of the team who assisted me through every step of my journey through publication of my book. Whenever I called or texted you with a question or concern, I always received a quick and thorough response. Thank you, Kym, for your patience with me and for always being there to encourage, advise, and direct me. I sincerely appreciate you.

To Jacqueline Flamm: many thanks for your patience and skills in teaching a "newbie" like me the difference between writing and writing a book. Thank you also, Jackie, for giving me your full attention and showing sincere appreciation for my writing. You inspired me to want to be an author, and you gave me the confidence I needed to become one. Thank you for treating me as if I were a "special somebody" with a gift. From the day we met, you made me feel I had a story worth telling—and that I truly have the talent to tell it. Jackie, I'm so grateful to you for all your encouragement, support, and tenacity. You were always available to me from the beginning to the end, and you made the entire process a fun, enriching experience.

Mike Aslett, thank you for your support, advice, warm spirit, and jovial manner. You were always willing to lend a helping hand, whether it was a general or technical request. I appreciate your dedication, your professional demeanor in the classroom, and your expertise as a production manager.

Thank you, Dina Forbes, for sharing your expertise with me. Dina, you are a true professional with excellent communication and editing skills. You're patient, you're tactful, you're a learned scholar, and you have a passion for your work. You often amazed me with your attention to detail and your thorough, intricate examination of text for appropriateness, correctness, and consistency. As with the other team members, I consider it a blessing from God that He placed you in my path to assist me in this phase of my life's journey. Words cannot express my gratitude for your expertise and help. I thank you, Dina, from the bottom of my heart.

To Marcelle Costanza: thank you, thank you, thank you for doing such an extraordinary job in designing the cover for this book. I continue to be amazed with your expertise as a professional graphic designer. We've been friends for more than twenty years, and throughout that time, you have willingly and expeditiously shared your skills by doing design work for me—whether it was to create a design, restore a photo, or remove images from an existing photo. I sincerely appreciate you, and I value our friendship. Thank you so much.

Thank you to Deborah A. Thompson, Vanya L. Williams, and Kimberly Evelyn for giving me feedback on my ideas, for your editing skills, and for encouraging me to write my book. I love you all so much, and I appreciate your standing by my side.

Thank you, Herby Augustin, for sharing your drawing skills with me. I'm grateful for your patience and endurance. I know it wasn't easy, considering the many changes we had to make. Thank you so much.

Special acknowledgment to my son-in-law, Hilery Williams Jr., my "ride or die" companion from the time my husband was murdered throughout my healing journey. I love you, Hilery.

Huge shout-outs to my Facebook family, my church family, and my friends for being my cheerleaders and motivating me to keep pressing on.

Thank you to my "gym buddies" at Planet Fitness (see page 103) for your encouragement and support—you know who you are. You gave me such a boost every time one of you would ask me, "How's the book coming along?" or refer to me as an author. These things made me happy and made me feel like a real author. A special thank-you to my gym buddy Liz Lashley for revealing to me and our gym buddies your recurring dream of my book being turned into a movie. It was truly uplifting the way you continued to share your dream with us. Hugs and kisses to all of you.

Thanks so much to *everyone* for your love and support throughout my journey of writing this book.

May God bless all of you and protect you in all that you do.

To God Be the Glory (TGBTG).

Introduction

Ever since I was young, the most important influence in my life has been my belief as a Christian and my high level of spirituality. I'm a very spiritual person, and for me, spirituality manifests itself as a belief and trust in God through Jesus Christ. I believe there is a direct revelation of God to the inner person through Jesus Christ and The Holy Spirit. *(God is Spirit, and those who worship Him must worship in spirit and truth.* [John 4:24]) So, we must seek God in spirit and in truth.

That belief is what spearheaded my search for truth in my childhood years. Jesus taught us that life isn't about just following the rules or mere behavior; it's much more than that. It's about living in the spirit behind the rules.

As humans, we unite with each other to bear fruit. To bear much fruit, we must walk in the spirit and have the spirit in us. *(Abide in me and I in you. As the branch cannot bear fruit of itself, unless it abides in the vine, neither can you, unless you abide in me.* [John 15:4])

To walk in the spirit, we must dialog with our Lord on a regular basis. We must pray the scriptures, which simply means communicating with God in his own words—to walk in the spirit, we must give His word back to Him by quoting scripture when we pray if we want to be reassured of His presence, His purpose, and His power. Prayer is not merely pleading our needs; it is claiming the provision that we have been offered a written contract. God wants us to quote His words back to Him, and He will fulfill His word. *(God must fulfill His word, because He is God and God cannot lie.* [Titus 1:2])

From the beginning of my life to the present, and certainly into the foreseeable future, one thing remains constant about me as a Black Christian woman: I am a spiritual being. Growing up as a Black person, I shared one everlasting belief with my family, my church family, and those I grew up with and around. It is a belief that comes from the core of our being; it always remains with us and sustains us. It is a belief in that which can only be perceived from within—from within our soul, not simply from our five senses. It is the belief that The Holy Spirit resides within each of us and will guide us in all that we do if we let Him.

So, when we communicate with God, we must listen to his voice for answers through The Holy Spirit. When we pray to God only about our damages and desires, we are throwing ourselves upon His mercy, which is a wonderful thing to do; however, when we pray God's promises, we hold His written word before our advocate in heaven, which ensures that our prayers are answered. Who is our advocate in heaven? Our advocate is Jesus Christ, our Lord.

So, where is this book taking you? It is taking you on an excursion to remind you that our journey here on earth can be mentally calm when we exercise our belief that The Holy Spirit lives within each of us and is here to be our helper, our comforter, and our guide. This book is a reminder to us that when we ask and believe, we will receive. *(Therefore, I tell you, whatever you ask for in prayer, believe that you have received it, and it will be yours.* [Mark 11:24])

From a metaphysical standpoint, I would be remiss if I didn't mention that this scripture from the Gospel of Mark is synonymous in meaning with the philosophy of the Law of Attraction: ask, believe, and receive.

I wrote this book for people who desire to understand the benefit of trusting and loving Christ despite the craziness of daily life. This book can teach you that we are all connected by the love and the spirit within us. And that God is in control of this connection through Jesus Christ and will always work for the greater good of us all. This book can show you that there is a creative process in God's plan for our lives and He will show us this plan if we establish and maintain an intimate relationship with Him through Jesus Christ and The Holy Spirit.

This book tells the story of how I recovered from tragedy through God's grace and mercy. In it, I'll share my story about how my belief in God, prayer, God's word, and The Holy Spirit collectively carried me through a horrific tragedy to a victorious and flourishing healing journey, culminating in a better way to live.

The Ever-Evolving Ella

I grew up with a strong sense of self. In hindsight, I think I always believed I could do whatever I set out to do. My behavior has been such that once I decide to do something, it will manifest itself in my life. In my younger years, I didn't realize my parents were my role models. I grew to understand that some years later.

My mother truly intrigued me. From a very young age, I remember I would follow her around the house just to see what she would do next. My father, on the other hand, was the one who made me feel special. He made me feel like I was one of a kind—like there was no other person like me in the whole wide world, and that I was an exceptional human being. He made me truly believe I was somebody important. That's probably the reason I was such an obedient child. My life's goal in those years was to please my parents. Even though we were very poor, I was rich in spirit, because I loved my parents and I knew they loved me. Their love fulfilled my soul. So, I was willing to do whatever they wanted me to do. I had such a burning desire to please them.

From the time I was about fourteen years old, I knew I was on a search for truth. I didn't know where to look for this "truth" or how to recognize it, but there was a yearning inside of me that told me I needed it. Before I was fourteen, I wasn't consciously aware that I wanted or needed this truth. But in my soul, there was always a longing for it. I felt compelled to fulfill "this thing" in me—this thing that I felt way deep down in the core of my being.

Now that I'm an adult, I realize that I initially found my truth by watching my mother, Margaret Estelle Branch. She was a quiet, modest, and sincere woman. She was truly amazing to me. I entertained myself by following her around the house—probably because she talked to herself all the time. And as a young child, I was very curious about why she did that. At first, it was entertaining. But then I began to wonder if my mother was crazy. I began to question what would make someone act that way. As I got a little older, there was a point in time when I became seriously concerned about my mother. I began to think she was having a nervous breakdown.

But as time passed, I came to realize that it wasn't true at all. In fact, she was an extremely intelligent, well-organized, and no-nonsense woman. She couldn't read or write, but she was always able to get credit from merchants to purchase the things she needed to sustain her life and the lives of her family. She used to call it buying things "on time." I remember so many times watching her make an X mark for her signature so she could make a purchase or pay a bill; then a family member would sign her name next to the X.

It was this woman, my mother, who laid the groundwork for the person I am today. I later discovered that during those times when I thought my mother was talking to herself, she wasn't talking to herself and wasn't crazy at all; she was praying and simply talking with God. She walked and talked with God all the time. And that's what was so amazing and amusing about her: she was always walking and talking—walking and talking around the house, walking and talking outside in the yard, or walking and talking while going up to what we called the "pig's pen."

The pig's pen was the place where daddy grew the hogs for "hog-killing time." After hog-killing time, we ate every part of the hog. We carved out the pork jowl from the pig's cheek to cook with our vegetables for seasoning. We made souse meat from the pig's feet, ears, tail, and parts of the head. Sometimes we pickled the feet or boiled them and then sautéed them with vinegar and hot sauce. We cleaned the intestines to make hog maws and chitterlings, a soul food delicacy. We used all the other parts of the hog for ham, pork chops, and so on. Our entire family looked forward to hog-killing time, because we always had plenty of food to eat. Even now, I feel a warm connection to those memories. As a matter of fact, about ten years prior to the death of my husband Willie, he and I started a tradition of cooking three things every New Year: souse meat, sweet potato pie, and black-eyed peas. Although Willie has been gone for several years now, I still follow our tradition by cooking these delicacies each New Year.

Through my mother's constant walking and talking with God, she taught me to believe in God because she made Him seem so real to me. She made Him seem like a real person. She taught me to go to church, to read my Bible, and to obey the Ten Commandments. She taught me to worship and praise God with the saints. Most of all, she taught me to always pray. She taught me that prayer really works. And that through prayer, we can develop that intimate relationship with our creator and learn of his grace and mercy, which will guide us through the tough times in our lives.

And this is how I get to the nucleus of my story. My story is really about my recovery from tragedy through God's grace and mercy.

At the time of this writing, it has been twelve years since the brutal murder of my dearly beloved husband, Deacon Willie R. Taylor, on May 7, 2007. My upbringing has afforded me the wherewithal to depend on God to sustain and direct my life all this time. He walked with me through my grief, my pain, and my sorrow. It is only because of God and His indwelling Holy Spirit that I remained functional and maintained such a high level of success during these years. God has walked with me every step of the way, and He has directed my path and talked with me just like He did with my mother. He even walked with me when I didn't know that I was walking…or that I was even alive. He told me when to go right and when to go left. He told me when to act and when to be still.

Two or three days after my husband's murder, God even told me who his murderer was. I remember it as if it were yesterday. I was staying at my daughter Vanya's home in Irvington, and I was sleeping that night with my granddaughter Jha'na. It was about 3 a.m. when I suddenly sat up erect in the bed. I shook Jha'na and told her, "Jha'na, Al-Rashad Benbow killed your grandfather. Jha'na, you know—the handyman who was working with him to renovate Aunt Jennie's house." Jha'na was groggy, and I knew she didn't understand me, but I simply had to tell someone. I believe God waited until I had come out of my zombie state to tell me, because then I had a clear-enough mind to listen and hear Him speak to me.

In the middle of the night, God revealed to me the identity of Willie's murderer.

Now I'll share with you my version of the events that have brought me to the time and space I'm in now.

Willie Disappears

On Monday, May 7, 2007, I woke up at my usual time. My husband, Willie, was still in bed. I got dressed, walked to the bed, kissed him goodbye, and went to work. Little did I know it would be the last time I would see my husband alive.

I left for work, kissing Willie goodbye for the last time.

My day started out fairly normal. I arrived at work at around 7 a.m., had my coffee, and started working at 8 a.m. as I always did. I called Willie at around noon to ask him if he'd be making any bank deposits that day, because I wanted to look over our bills for the month during my lunchtime and pay whatever I could. Willie told me he was on Tillinghast Street in Newark, NJ, where he was doing some renovations on his Aunt Jennie's home. I got the impression that he was distracted and that someone was with him.

At one point, Willie asked me to hold on. When he returned, I said to him, "It sounds like you're really busy." I don't recall him responding to my statement. So, I said, "Well, I won't keep you on the phone. I just want to know if you're making any bank deposits today." He told me he'd be depositing $2,000 in cash, a $500 check, and two other small checks from accounting clients. "Okay, thanks, Sweetie," I said. "See you at home tonight."

I got home at around 6 p.m. Willie and I were planning to go shopping at 8 p.m. to get a new pink carpet for our guest bedroom. Willie was always on time for things we had scheduled. So, when he still wasn't home by 8:30 p.m., I tried to reach him on his cell phone. When he didn't answer, I continued to call him. It wasn't until around 1 a.m. that someone answered his phone. I couldn't decipher the voice, but hearing someone answer made me hopeful. Yet at the same time, it worried me. Right away, I called my daughter Vanya. Both she and my son-in-law, Hilery, were shocked because they knew Willie well and knew he always came home when he was expected—he never stayed out very late, never mind all night. We talked for a few minutes, and they tried to reassure me. Before we got off the phone, they asked me to keep them informed and to let them know if they could do anything for me.

For the next several hours, I kept trying to reach Willie by phone, but to no avail. I finally went to sleep at around 4 a.m.

As soon as I got up for work the next morning, I called Vanya again. I don't recall our conversation—I may have been in shock at the time—but she filled in the details afterward.

According to Vanya's account, I called her at around 5:30 a.m. and asked her how long it would take for the authorities to tell a person that a missing loved one is dead.

When she questioned why I was asking, I told her, "Because Willie didn't come home at all last night, and he's never done that in the 23 years we've been married. I think he may be dead."

"Well, maybe he fell asleep," my daughter suggested, to which I responded, "Willie has never not come home. You know the kind of husband he is. He's a very upstanding man and would never stay out all night. And if he was sleepy, he would've checked in with me to let me know what was going on."

I remember telling her I was very worried because it was so out of character for him. Finally, I told her I was just going to work as I always did and would see what happens.

My daughter Debbie, who lives in Virginia, later told me her perspective of what happened that morning. She was awakened by a call on her cell phone at around 8 a.m. and noticed she had missed several earlier telephone calls from her sister. Concerned, she immediately called Vanya, who told her Willie hadn't returned home the night before.

"Well, maybe his truck broke down," Debbie offered.

But Vanya responded that the state troopers had been checking Willie's usual route and had seen no sign of his vehicle. She told Debbie that I'd gone to work because I wasn't able to think straight, so the two sisters agreed to check in later and Debbie called me right away.

"What's going on?" she asked me.

I told her that Willie hadn't come home and we couldn't find any trace of him.

Debbie asked me if anyone had filed a missing person report, and I responded that I was informed I'd have to wait 24 hours before filing one. She pointed out that it was past the 24-hour waiting period, and she suggested to Vanya's husband Hilery that he and I go to the police station to file the report.

I kept myself busy at work until Hilery called me at 9 a.m. to tell me he was coming to pick me up and we were going to find my husband. While my daughters were calling hospitals, police, and anyone else they could think of in New Jersey and the surrounding areas, Hilery and I went to the local police stations in Irvington and other surrounding towns to find any information we could, but to no avail. Exasperated, we ultimately filed the missing person report in East Orange. It seemed as though Willie had just disappeared from the face of the earth—vanished into thin air.

After filing the report, Hilery and I sat in his truck and discussed the situation for a few minutes, trying to decide what to do next. Hilery felt very strongly about going back to Newark to look for Willie again since it was the last known place of his whereabouts. He told me he'd gone to Tillinghast Street in Newark before he picked me up but left when he didn't see Willie's red Jeep there.

Because of Willie's high blood pressure, Debbie suggested he could've had a stroke or some other health problem and then someone stole the Jeep, so we all decided Hilery and I would check Tillinghast Street again in case Willie was still in the house.

Finding Willie

Hilery and I got to Tillinghast Street at around noon. Hilery called Debbie and told her that we still didn't see Willie's Jeep but that neither of us had a key to the house, so Debbie said we should just break the door down and she'd accept responsibility for any damages. "Just call me when you know something, because my nerves are a wreck," she added. "I'm going to the store to get me some cigarettes."

Hilery began looking for ways to get in to the house, but the front and side doors were locked. He went to the back of the house, where he knew Willie and his assistant were upgrading the entrance to the basement. From the entrance to the basement in the backyard, Hilery called to me where I stood on the driveway, about ten feet away. He told me he could see a tarp that seemed to be covering something. I suggested he move it, and when he did, he discovered that the tarp was covering a hole leading to the back door entrance to the basement. "There are no steps," he called to me. "It's about five feet deep. I can jump in, but I don't know if I'll be able to get out."

"Are you sure you want to jump in there, Hil?" I called back. "You might get hurt." Before I could get an answer, he had jumped into the hole.

All I can remember hearing Hilery say is, "Oh, s***—it's Wil! You cannot come down here and see this. It's horrible!"

"Let me in! Let me in! I must get in!" I immediately yelled back to him, panicked. "Go through the basement and let me in the side door!"

I know now that I was hysterical. Finally, Hilery made it to the side door and let me in. I was screaming, "Lord Jesus, where is he? Where is he?" Hilery told me Willie was on the floor in the basement, so I ran down the steps to the basement and…no! There was my husband on the floor! He was on his back, facing the ceiling.

Hilery later told me he'd found Willie face-down in a mound of dirt on the concrete floor and had turned him face-up to see if he was alive, which is when he saw that Willie wasn't breathing and his face was bashed in.

The Murder Scene

The murder scene was a gruesome sight. Seeing the man I had loved for 23 years lying on that concrete basement floor was horrifying. I ran to him, knelt on the floor beside him, and leaned over him. My hands went directly to his face. He was as stiff as a board.

I leaned over Willie's body, touching his face.

In that moment, everything changed for me. Maybe that was the moment I went into shock, because it was all so unreal. It seemed like a nightmare, as if I were watching a horror film. I couldn't believe it was my husband lying on the concrete floor before me, his face—especially around his right eye—a mass of dried blood. (His right eyeball was never found.) I kept touching and patting his face and upper body as if expecting him to respond. But his face and his whole body were so hard. I refused to believe he wasn't going to just wake up. I remember thinking, "Is it really Willie? Maybe it's someone else. Why won't he move?" I continued to pat his body through his clothing. Hoping, just hoping. I don't really know what I was hoping for—maybe that Willie would just get up off that floor and speak to me, and everything would go back to the way it was.

This went on for some time—I don't know how long. Then I felt someone touch my shoulder. It was a paramedic. "Miss, you have to leave," he said. "But I can't leave," I told him. "I need to stay here with my husband. He needs me. Somebody has to stay with him. He can't just stay here by himself. He's my husband." After much pleading, they could see the state I was in and simply took me by my arm and escorted me out of the house.

The next thing I remember is standing outside on the side of the street opposite the house, facing the front door. Other people were already standing there. There was yellow crime scene barricade tape across the entire front of the property. I waited out on the street for hours. It seemed like an eternity.

Hilery had already notified EMS. EMS notified Newark's police department, who notified the crime scene investigators' office, prosecutor's office, homicide department, and Essex County medical examiner's office.

I don't recall anything from the time I first saw my husband lying on that concrete floor with his face bashed in until I had a sudden awareness that Hilery and a few others, including Rev. Dr. Perry Simmons, Jr., the pastor of my church, were standing alongside me. And although both Hilery and Pastor Simmons later told me that I had called Pastor Simmons earlier, I don't remember making the phone call.

We stood there waiting for what seemed like forever for the paramedics to bring Willie out of the house. Little by little, more family, friends, church members, and other onlookers joined us. Then Al-Rashad Benbow, Willie's hired helper who had been working with him to renovate the basement, walked up to me. He seemed to appear out of nowhere. "I'm sorry," he told me. I don't remember whether I responded to him, but I do recall that I made eye contact with him. I wanted to ask him some questions—questions like whether he had been with Willie at around noon the day before. I thought it would be the start of a conversation, but he disappeared while I was getting my thoughts together.

A few seconds later, I remember seeing him crossing the street and then walking up the street away from us. "Why is he leaving?" I thought. "He should be standing here with us for Willie. He should be talking to me about Willie. My God, he worked here with Willie—why is he not concerned enough to stand with us and talk to me?"

As time went on, I realized that no one was talking much. We all just stood there, waiting, anticipating. I remember suddenly hearing myself say to Pastor Simmons, "Oh my goodness, now I don't have a husband." I guess some sense of reality was starting to sink in. "I must have a husband. Now I have to get another husband." I think I was half out of my mind and in a terrible state of shock. I don't know why I said it, and I don't know why I remember it. But in hindsight, I think I had a sudden realization that Willie was dead, and I couldn't imagine being alone.

It seemed as if we stood there on the street for several hours. I remember that Pastor Simmons never left my side. He just stood there with me, most of the time saying very little. That was a huge comfort to me. He stayed with us until they finally brought Willie out on the stretcher, covered up. I believe that's when I knew he was dead. The ambulance started up and drove Willie away…to the morgue. Willie was pronounced dead at 1406 hours by Dr. Grayson of the University of Medicine and Dentistry of New Jersey (UMDNJ) University Hospital. The crowd disbursed.

Meanwhile, in Virginia, Debbie returned home from getting cigarettes. Her husband, Johnell, met her in their front hallway with tears in his eyes. It stopped her in her tracks. "What is it, Johnell? What's wrong?" she asked him.

"Debbie, somebody killed him," he replied. "Man…somebody killed Wil!"

"No! No! No!" Debbie screamed. She ran to call Hilery, who told her about what he had found.

Debbie told me later that she had tried to talk to me but that I was making no sense and seemed to be in a state of shock. She kept me on the phone with her until she confirmed that Pastor Simmons was at the scene with me. Then she started calling friends and loved ones in Virginia, including the pastor of her church, my sister Marie, and my nieces Trese and Teisha. And Trese went to the school to pick up Debbie's daughter, Zsa. Soon, Debbie and Johnell's home was packed with people. The two of them and Zsa were numb, angry, confused, and heartbroken—seemingly all in one emotion.

Debbie later explained that she had a sudden awareness: "I have to get to my mother right now!"

They immediately started to prepare for their drive from Virginia to New Jersey, leaving the next morning. The trip was basically silent—they didn't know what to do, what to say, or what to expect when they got to my home.

The Aftermath

After Hilery and I left the murder scene, I remember us going downtown to the police station, where my daughter Vanya met us. We had to complete the incident report, and the officer who talked with us advised us to reach out to an organization called Families of Victims of Violent Crimes. The officer gave us the name and contact information of the detective assigned to the case, suggesting we call the detective if we had questions.

I called James Ronald Curry, who owns the Plinton Curry Funeral Homes, Inc. and is a member of my church, the Abyssinian Baptist Church (ABC) in Newark. We made plans for him to pick Willie's body up from the morgue, prepare his body for the funeral, and handle all the funeral arrangements. Ron contacted me once he had Willie's body in his possession.

Later that night, Debbie and her family arrived from Virginia. I don't remember much about that night except that we were all at Vanya's house in Irvington. So many people stopped by to pay their respects, bring us food, and ask what they could do to help us. At that time, I felt like there was nothing and no one that could make me feel better. I said a silent prayer: "God help me!"

That Thursday, Debbie and Vanya worked diligently to put together a notification list for our family, friends, and Willie's business associates to inform them about Willie's murder and funeral. We all sat around the dining room table at my home. I did my best when my daughters asked me for information about various people's names, but my input was minimal because I was so distraught and lost in a sort of zombie zone. I now believe I was in an enormous state of shock.

It was very important to Debbie and Vanya that they notify everyone who needed to know, because they knew Willie was valued by so many people. He had many professional and personal affiliations, because not only was he a financial advisor and tax accountant with a widespread clientele, but he was a deacon at the ABC serving the Newark community and was heavily involved in missionary work in Essex and Somerset Counties.

So, my daughters took the task very seriously and compiled a contact list that ultimately consisted of about 400 people. They decided to designate specific individuals to contact others within a group—for example, Willie's friends from AT&T, Willie's family in Georgia, my family in New York and Virginia, Willie's clientele, his business associates in World Financial Group (WFG), and HomeSharing, the group he did volunteer work with. That gave Debbie and Vanya a level of comfort that they had reached as many people as possible to tell them about the arrangements for the celebration of Willie's life.

◆

The Newark Police Department's incident report of Willie's murder (page 1 of 2).

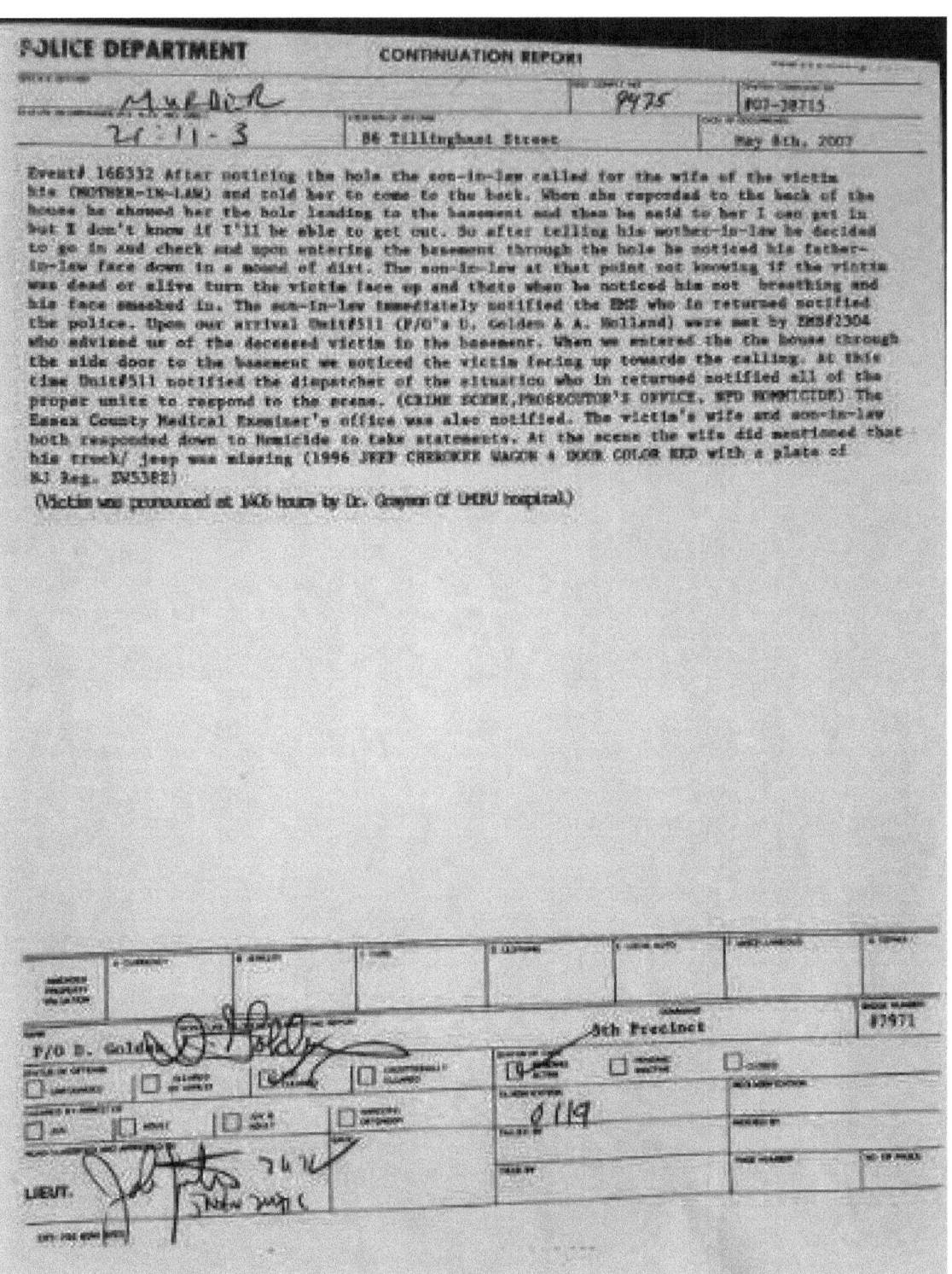

The Newark Police Department's incident report of Willie's murder (page 2 of 2).

Somerset County man slain in Newark

By Peggy Ackermann/Statehouse Bureau

A Somerset County man was found bludgeoned to death this afternoon in the basement of a house he owned in Newark, police said.

Family members discovered the body of Willie Taylor, 67, of Hillsborough in the Tillinghast Street house at about 1:30 p.m., Detective Todd McClendon said.

In addition, Taylor's car, a red 1996 Jeep Cherokee with New Jersey license plates, was missing. Newark police gave the license plate number as ZW5-38Z.

Taylor was in the habit of working in the basement of the house where his body was found, the detective added.

Police did not release additional details about death, and they did not announce the arrest of any suspects.

Contributed by George Berkin
May 8, 2007
From NJ.com; available at: www.nj.com/ ledgerupdates/2007/05/ somerset_county_man_slain_in_n.html

Booker lashes out against Newark crime

In speech at police graduation, mayor compares situation to war

Newark Mayor Cory Booker set out to inspire a group of rookie officers during a police graduation ceremony yesterday at City Hall.

But during the fiery speech that ended with a rousing ovation, Booker also vented his anger with the continued level of deadly violence that claimed three lives this week.

A 69-year-old man was strangled in his North Ward home, a 67-year-old church deacon was bludgeoned in the Tillinghast Street house he was renovating, and a 39-year-old ex-con was shot to death on South Ninth Street.

Booker said the killings had him "twisted up." Shouting and slamming his fists into the podium, he compared the war in Iraq to the battle against crime back home. "We have a war here in Newark. We have our challenges here. We have our fight right here," he said.

The three deaths brought the number of murders so far this year in Newark to 35, police said. As of yesterday, that number was slightly more than the same period in 2006, when the city murder rate hit a 16-year high.

The week's first victim, Miguel Rodriguez, 69, was found by a neighbor Monday night lying on the floor of his Bloomfield Avenue home, the back door wide open, authorities said. Authorities aren't sure how long he'd been there, but an autopsy determined that he'd been strangled.

The next day, Willie Taylor's wife and son-in-law found him lying face down in the basement of a Tillinghast Street house he was renovating for renters, his face bashed in an apparent robbery, authorities said.

A few hours later, at 10:45 p.m., Steven Strickland, 39, was shot to death on South Ninth Street. Witnesses said he'd been fighting with someone just before he was killed.

Although Booker was angered by all the killings, he singled out the "slaughter" of Taylor as particularly galling.

An accountant and deacon at Abyssinian Baptist Church on West Kinney Street, Taylor grew up in the Newark area but lived for many years in Hillsborough with his wife, Ella.

The Rev. Perry Simmons of Abyssinian Baptist Church said Taylor visited the sick and disabled on behalf of the congregation and served as a spiritual adviser to its ministers.

"He was one of my right-hand men," Simmons said.

Taylor started Monday collecting rent from tenants at another home they owned in Irvington. Then he went to the Tillinghast house, where he was renovating the basement.

After he failed to return home that night, his wife and son-in-law started searching for him. They reported him missing to police in East Orange, where he'd last been seen by a partner at his financial planning office, Ella Taylor said.

Taylor's son-in-law, Hilery Williams, later found him face down in the basement on Tillinghast Street. His laptop, checkbook, $2,200 in collected rent and his Jeep Cherokee were gone, his family said.

"He was just a marvelous guy," Ella Taylor said yesterday. "He was a good person and did not deserve this kind of treatment."

By Jonathan Schuppe
May 10, 2007
From *The Star-Ledger*

The Funeral

On Friday, May 11, our immediate family was asked to go to the Plinton Curry Funeral Home in Westfield to view Willie's body. Our entire family went. When we arrived, Ron Curry, the owner, suggested we prepare ourselves before we go into the room. When Ron opened the door, some of the women—including me—had much difficulty standing, and the men were trying to hold us upright. Willie's face looked very fleshy, much like chopped meat. He was slaughtered. Ron later told me he had to rebuild Willie's face in order to have an open-casket funeral. Remember—his murderer bludgeoned his face with a hammer, and one of his eyes was never found. Ron had Willie's neck resting on a brick brace. His face was unrecognizable, so we visually examined his feet to confirm that it was him. All of Willie's family knew his feet had a distinct look because of the frostbite he'd gotten when he was serving in the military. Between his stature and the evidence of the frostbite, we were satisfied that it was him. Some of the women became so overwhelmed that they had to leave the room. But I stayed. I felt I just needed to be near him. Maybe I was less disturbed by the sight than the other women were because I had already seen him in the house the day we found him—I'm not sure. Eventually, we all had to leave because it was so difficult for us to see him that way.

The next day, Debbie and Vanya worked diligently in researching and compiling all the information the family wanted to include in the program for Willie's going-home service. In my opinion, the program was perfect. I don't remember giving my daughters any input for it, but they told me I wrote a poem to Willie, which they included in the program. When they finished compiling the information, they gave it to Ron for publication.

Celebrating The Life of
Deacon Willie R. Taylor
June 28th, 1939 - May 8th, 2007

Friday, May 18th, 2007
11:00 am
Abyssinian Baptist Church
224 West Kinney Street, Newark, NJ
Rev. Dr. Perry Simmons, Jr., Pastor

The program for Willie's going-home service (cover).

Obituary

Deacon Willie R. Taylor was born on June 28th, 1939 in Cuthbert Georgia to the late Roosevelt and Flora Taylor. Willie Attended the Cuthbert School system and graduated from Randolph High School in Cuthbert, Ga. Willie was a boxer in his youth and later went on to join the Army Airbourne division and served his country proudly on the home front during the Vietnam conflict from September 5th, 1961 until September 4th, 1964. In the military Willie earned many honorable decorations. Willie graduated from Florida A&M in Tallahassee in 1971 with a Bachelor's degree in Accounting. Before settling in Hillsborough, Willie also lived in Plainfield and Irvington. Willie Married Ella Branch in 1984 and together they have spent the last 22 years of their lives in Hillsborough. Willie had been employed as a Corporate Tax accountant for the past 30 years, but most recently he had employed with World Financ ial Group for the last 8 years, and loved his job dearly. Willie and Ella joined Abyssinian Baptist together in 1986 and Willie became a Deacon in 19___. Willie was a member of World Financial Group, and 82nd Airbourne. He was a charitable person being involved in the PAL, Danny Thomas Foundation amongst others. Willie was a volunteer for Somerset County Home Sharing. Willie was some many things to so many people including chef, spiritual advisor. Willie was preceeded in death his Mother Flora Elizabeth Taylor, Father Roosevelt Taylor, Uncle Willie Fred Grubbs, Brother Willie James Taylor, and his Sister Annie Frances Mitchell.

To Cherish his memory he leaves his loving and devoted Wife Ella W. Taylor, Daughters Deborah W. Thompson (Johnell Thompson) of Petersburg, Va, and Va'nya L. Williams

(Hilery Williams, Jr.) of Irvington, NJ. Sons Josepheus Kenneth Taylor of Atlanta, Ga, Vincent Fitzgerald Taylor of Cuthbert, Ga, and Mario Xavier Taylor of Atlanta, Ga. Sisters Eva Mae taylor of Cuthbert, Ga, Versie Moore of Augusta, Ga, and Gloria Williams-Way (James Way) of Augusta, Ga. Brothers Nathaniel Taylor (Patricia Taylor) of Atlanta, Ga, and Johnny Taylor (Diane Taylor), of Augusta, Ga. Sisters-in-Law Estelle marie Stewart (Moses) of Ettrick, Va, Martha Scott (Charles) of Ettrick, Va, Toresa Diane Lee of Peterson, Va. Brothers-in-Law Mitchell Romaine Branch of Omaha, Nebraska, and Wallace Earl Branch (Ruth) of Jamaica Queens, NY. 7 grandchildren, 1 great Grand daughter, devoted cousins and a host of aunts, unc les, nieces, nephews, and special friends John McNally and John B. Watts both of New Jersey.

The program for Willie's going-home service (page 2).

The program for Willie's going-home service (page 3).

Order of Service

Prelude……………………………………………..Hymn-Music only

Processional…………………...............Music (Entrance of Family and Friends)

Hymn of Comfort "The Lord's Prayer"……..Gloria Parker

Scripture Reading

                              Old Testament

                              New Testament

Prayer of Consolation

Solo "Praise The Lord, I'm Free"……………..Gloria Parker

Reflections……………………………………..Deacon Earl Williams
                                                Chairman of the Deacon Board

Special Tribute By: Granddaughters
"The World's Greatest"……..............................Kayla Williams
                                                Lsahnelle Thompson
                                                Jhana Lovett

Eulogy…………………………………………........Rev. Perry Simmons

Recessional

Attending Nurse- Sylvia Sherrod
Pianist- Gloria Parker

Active Pallbearers
Mario Taylor
Vincent Taylor
Hilery Williams
Johnell Thompson
Reggie
Wallace Branch
John B. Watts
John McNally

Honorary Pallbearers
Kayla Williams
Zsahnelle Thompson
Jhana Lovett
Kenya Spenser
Vermekia Taylor
Kianna Spenser
Jasmine Barnett
Tiffany Woolford
Shawntee' Eutsy
India Williams

Ushers
Terrell Lovett
E. Jevon Eutsy
Greg Taylor
Richard Taylor
Roger C. Brown
Charles Scott

The program for Willie's going-home service (page 4).

A Tribute to Willie Roosevelt Taylor "Jr."
A Better Place

There is a place that you have never seen,
beyond this world you know.
A place that you have only heard of, but someday hope to go.
It is not on any map; it is far beyond the stars.
There are no roads to take you there, just love, trust, and scars.
It is a home purchased by Jesus' own blood,
my what a wonderful story.
Because of His great mercy and love,
I can wait for you in glory.

This is a place of perfect peace, where hearts are free from care.
It is a tabernacle of beauty, bliss, and joy that is beyond compare.
And though I understand that many hearts are
saddened because I had to leave.
God called, and I could not stay another day,
so understand this please.
Live not in constant grief that I am gone from sight.
Approach each day with thankfulness for me
and faith to stay in the fight.

One day, we will meet again
on heaven's celestial shore.
But take comfort that I am with you in spirit,
wherever you may go.
So cherish each time you pray, hold a hand,
or see a snowflake fall.
Know that memories and my soul allow me
to answer when you call.
I leave a lasting legacy of faith, hope, love, and loyalty.
So face each day with pride, grace, perseverance and dignity.

When it is time for you to travel here,
I know that you will wear a smile,.
As you leave a world of pain, grief, hate, and
strife to traverse that final mile.
So I say goodbye to those I love but only for a while.
For, I have gone the way that each heart
must walk alone, as God claims His child.
But Jesus waits with outstretched arms and
loved ones welcome me home.
And, I am right there with you, so take
solace in knowing that you are not alone.

Gloria Taylor Williams-Way

The program for Willie's going-home service (page 5).

DEAR WIL,

AS I SPEAK INTO YOUR PRESENCE, I GREET YOU WITH A KISS, AS I ALWAYS DID, AND I HEAR YOU SAY "HI HONEY".

AS I SPEAK INTO YOUR PRESENCE, I TELL YOU THIS TERRIBLE THING THAT HAPPENED TO YOU HAS AFFECTED THE LIVES OF ALL WHO KNEW YOU AND EVEN THOSE WHO DID NOT KNOW YOU,

AS I SPEAK INTO YOUR PRESENCE, I TELL YOU THAT THE LOVE YOU GAVE TO SO MANY IS BEING GIVEN BACK TO ME.

AS I SPEAK INTO YOUR PRESENCE, I TELL YOU THAT THE MEMORY OF YOU IS CEMENTED INTO THE HEARTS OF ALL.

AS I SPEAK INTO YOUR PRESENCE, I TELL YOU OF THE OUTPOURING OF CONDOLENCES FROM FAMILY AND FRIENDS FAR AND NEAR DATING AS FAR BACK AS OUR YEARS AT BELL LABORATORIES.

AS I SPEAK INTO YOUR PRESENCE, I TELL YOU HOW ALL THE RELATIONSHIPS YOU BUILT ARE REACHING OUT TO ME TO ASSIST ME IN MY STRUGGLE TO CONTINUE MY LIFE WITHOUT YOU.

SO DON'T WORRY ABOUT ME BECAUSE YOUR SUPPORT TEAM IS ON THE JOB!

WE ALL KNOW THAT "WITHIN EVERY ADVERSITY LIES THE SEED OF AN EQUIVILENT ADVANTAGE"......

YOUR DEDICATION TO OTHERS IS THAT EQUIVILENT ADVANTAGE THAT HAS TAKEN ROOT AND IS EXPLODING AS A FOREST.

I KNOW THAT YOU ARE ABSENT FROM US....... BUT YOU ARE FREE, HAPPY AND PEACEFUL IN YOUR PRESENCE WITH OUR LORD.

I LOVE YOU, ETERNALLY

YOUR WIFE, ELLA

Professional Services Entrusted to

Plinton Curry Funeral Homes, Inc.

James Ronald Curry, BA, LFD - NJLIC #4053
Manager / CEO
(908) 232-6869 - www.plintoncurry.com

The program for Willie's going-home service (page 6).

◆

I was in regular contact with Ron during the preparation of Willie's body for the funeral. Ron was Willie's friend, and we all attended the same church. My family and I were adamant about having an open casket, because we needed to see Willie one last time. So, to prepare Willie's body for the funeral, Ron had to rebuild his face. One night at around 11 p.m., a week or so after Ron picked up Willie's body, he called me and told me he had been working diligently all day and into the night trying to recreate Willie's facial features. "I'm not going to leave here tonight until I see Willie," he said. He did a great job, and he even gave us a video of all the stages of the reconstruction so we could clearly see all the work that had gone into the final product.

Because my son-in-law, Johnell, was very close to Willie, we asked him to choose Willie's outfit for the funeral. He tried so hard, but going through Willie's clothing was very emotional for him. Soon he began to feel dizzy and show other signs that something was wrong. When my neighbor checked Johnell's blood pressure and we discovered that it had escalated to over 200, we told Johnell to relax while the rest of us worked together to choose an outfit suitable for the burial. We now realize how serious Johnell's condition was and that we should have taken him to the hospital, but at the time, nobody recognized the urgency. It's just one example of the stress and heartache Willie's death brought to our family.

◆

Willie was laid to rest on May 18. I don't remember everything about that day—I was in a sort of fog. But I knew the funeral was about to happen, so I set my mind as best I could to get ready for it. I was able to pick out something to wear, but I wasn't functioning as I normally did. I was inattentive and distracted. Now in hindsight, I can see that I was in a very fragile and emotional state—just going through the motions.

I chose my pretty, lacy, three-piece black outfit that was one of Willie's favorites: a skirt, a blouse, and a jacket with hints of gold thread intertwined within the material. I felt good about my selection and was confident about how I looked in it. I hoped Willie would notice me as he always did when I looked good and that he would compliment me. I dressed for Willie that day. It was one of my fantasy moments.

By the time I was ready, I noticed that my entire family was already waiting for me in the den. We went outside, where Ron and his staff were waiting for us. He had two limousines lined up, along with family vehicles ready to make the one-hour trip from my home in Hillsborough to my church in Newark. Under the direction of Rev. Rahmin Wynn, we loaded up and started the caravan. As I remember, it was a bit of a challenge to keep us together as we drove on Route 287 North and Route 78 East, both known to be busy highways. I remember that at one point, Rev. Wynn had to stop the caravan, get out, get us all together again, and establish some traveling rules.

Our trip to Newark took more than an hour, but we made it there safely. When we entered the church, Ron's crew was waiting for us. The church was packed. It looked as if all 400 of the people my daughters had notified were present, along with their friends. We were greeted by eight beautiful 36 x 24 x 36 young ladies dressed in black from head to toe: elegant, lacy dresses; lace stockings; and fancy, flamboyant hats. They were truly a sight to behold—the epitome of class. And as we found out later, they were the chauffeurs who would drive us to the gravesite in those shiny black limousines.

One of the fashionable chauffeurs from the Plinton Curry Funeral Home.

More of the chauffeurs.

As the processional music played, the beautiful ladies ushered our family to their seats. They carried out their duties in a very sophisticated manner. To add to this display of class, the pallbearers and ushers wore black tuxedos. The entire ceremony was very upscale, with style and appeal. Huge posters depicting various times in Willie's life were displayed across the entire length of the pulpit and around the church. (See some of those pictures in his obituary.) It was as if he was there; it all made him truly come alive to me. Many family members agreed—we could definitely feel his presence.

Pastor Simmons presented the eulogy, describing what a fine man Willie had been. He noted that Willie had served on the home front in the United States Army during the

Vietnam War and was a member of the 82nd Airborne Division. He talked about Willie's work at the Abyssinian Baptist Church, visiting the sick on behalf of the ABC congregation, serving as a spiritual advisor to the ABC ministers, and generously providing financial support to the church. At one point, he described Willie as one of his "right-hand men." After the eulogy, an invitation was extended to those who wished to share some words with us about Willie. Willie's youngest sister, Gloria, quickly arose and accepted the offer. Others followed.

After the tributes, attendees were invited to view Willie's body. I remember that Willie's Aunt Jennie and I were asked to approach the casket first to say goodbye. It was difficult for both of us, but we got through it and then returned to our seats. After everyone was given the opportunity to say goodbye, according to tradition, our oldest child, Debbie, was ushered up to close the casket. Debbie was very nervous and said she wasn't aware ahead of time that she'd be asked to do that. She told us that they put her hand on the lever to close the casket and that she kept taking her hand back because she didn't want to be the last to say goodbye to her dad. Finally, they forcefully made her close the casket, which she said was a very heartfelt and exhausting experience for her.

The men, adorned in their chic black attire as they carried Willie's casket, led the processional out of the church. Ron's Cadillac Escalade flatbed truck was ready to transport Willie's body to Fairmount Cemetery in East Orange for his military funeral.

Per tradition, to honor the memory of Willie's service to his country, a United States flag was draped over Willie's closed casket. After farewell words were spoken, honor guards from the United States Army fired three volleys from rifles. Then the flag was removed from the casket, folded in a highly symbolic ceremony, and presented to me.

United States Army Honor Guards presented the flag to me.

Finally, the casket was lowered into the ground. It was a very sad moment for me, my family, and Willie's family. We all stood there for some time with the realization that this, in fact, was the end of the physical Willie, although he would continue to live in the hearts of us all.

I immediately felt a hole inside of me, knowing part of me was gone. There was a vacant space I had to fill if I was to continue with a productive life. But I now know that the Holy Spirit, my comforter, was there ready to help me deal with that vacant space and propel me forward to my future endeavors.

The repast was held at the Abyssinian Baptist Church, where Willie's family and friends celebrated his life and our love for him in the midst of his death. I was still in somewhat of a daze, but I do remember that many people participated, including a large number of family and friends from Virginia, Georgia, Maryland, and New York. This, again, reminded us all that Willie had touched the lives of so many people.

This flag from Willie's casket is proudly displayed in my living room.

Why the Murder?

The day after Willie was laid to rest, our family and friends gathered at my home for a going-home celebration of Willie's life. It was a beautiful celebration, with many people in attendance. We all talked with each other, sharing fond memories of Willie. Each of us had a story to share about some kind thing he had done for us, some words of encouragement he had offered, or some challenging counsel he had given—he was very good at giving counsel. It was a wonderful way to honor and commemorate him.

With the funeral behind us, it was time for the family to move forward. So, our next priority was to find out who murdered Willie.

Why would anyone murder Willie? He was a peaceful man. A man of God. A man who loved his fellow man. A man who was always ready to reach out and help someone else. He would always volunteer to help with community functions and be of service to those in the community, especially the underprivileged. He was always doing something to help people he felt were less fortunate than he was. His last good deed before his death was to help the husband of a temporary employee (a "temp") I worked with at Rutgers University in Newark. The fact that it was his last good deed was significant because it was the same good deed that led to his demise.

One day when I was on break in the coffee room, I started talking with the temp. She seemed to be a nice person. I had seen her around the office before, but she and I worked under different directors, so I had only spoken to her in passing until that day. She was a tall Black woman, very personable and friendly, so talking with her was easy. Also, I have always felt a personal responsibility to converse and share my life experiences, when possible, with younger women and mentor them whenever I have the opportunity.

At some point in our conversation, the temp mentioned that she didn't have a ride home that day, and she asked me if I could give her a ride. She told me she didn't live far from our office. I told her my husband was picking me up that day and that I didn't think he'd mind, but that I would ask him when he arrived. She appeared relieved.

The temp and I coordinated our leaving time and left the office together that day. Once we approached the car, I introduced her to Willie and asked him if we could give her a ride home. "Sure," Willie said. He was very cordial to her, which was his usual manner. After all, he was accustomed to interacting with people. As a financial planner, tax accountant, and insurance salesman, Willie had many clients. He was a very social person with great communication skills. So, right away, he and the temp began to chat—mostly about general topics. Then she asked Willie about his vocation. He told her the many things he was involved in, including being a landlord. She told Willie that her husband was out of work and needed a job, and she asked if Willie could help him. Willie told her he would try, and he gave her his phone number so he could speak with her husband directly. Willie was renovating his Aunt Jennie's home, and he figured he might need a handyman to help him.

Al-Rashad Benbow, the temp's husband, called Willie a few days later. Willie told him he needed someone to help him renovate the home of his aunt, who was living in a nursing facility and wanted to rent out her house. Benbow was excited, and he started working right away. I remember that Willie had some complaints about the quality of Benbow's work right from the beginning. He also told me later that Benbow was frequently asking for advances on his pay. Being the kindhearted person that he was, Willie overlooked Benbow's poor quality of work and continued to give him pay advances. I believe Willie felt it was his way to "give back" to someone less fortunate than he was.

In an effort to help Benbow increase his income, Willie decided to involve him and his wife in the World Financial Group business. WFG is a very intricate business dealing with marketing, investments, and insurance. To be successful at it, a person would need to pass a challenging test and qualify for a state license. I told Willie I didn't feel that Benbow and his wife were good candidates for the WFG business, but he insisted on giving them a chance. So we scheduled a night meeting for the four of us at their home. We spent a couple of hours discussing the WFG process and explained what they would have to do to make the business successful. Using charts and calculations, we showed them what they needed to do to make a good income, and we told them they'd have to follow the plan. They were excited, so we scheduled a date for them to attend an official WFG meeting in our office in Fairfield. We felt it would give them the opportunity to hear an official presentation, get a second overview of the business, and meet other members of WFG Team.

They attended the scheduled meeting, but Willie was very disappointed and embarrassed because during the break and every chance he could get, Benbow spent it trying to borrow money from the WFG members and guests. So, Willie realized I was right about not involving him in WFG. I believe Benbow had never been in such a setting with so many apparently affluent people, so he got very excited and possibly figured they would hand out money to him just like Willie did.

One Sunday night a few weeks later, Willie and I were sitting in the den just relaxing and chitchatting. I noticed that Willie's mind seemed to wander all of a sudden. So, I asked him if there was something wrong. He told me he thought perhaps Benbow was using drugs because he would disappear for long periods of time during the workday and he continuously asked for pay advances. "He seems to need so much extra money," Willie told me, adding that some of his tools were missing and no one had been on premises except the two of them.

I was flabbergasted and frightened at the same time. I felt very afraid for Willie to be alone with a person of this caliber, especially since Willie believed Benbow was using drugs and we didn't know him very well. Remember, at this time, we had known him for only a few months. So, I asked Willie to promise me he wouldn't be alone with Benbow at all anymore. I told him I felt it was dangerous and possibly a threat to his life. I reiterated it more than once because I was afraid for his safety and felt very strongly about it. I wanted it to be clear to Willie that I felt he was in danger being alone with Benbow.

"I think I need to let him go," Willie told me, which indicated that he had heard and understood me.

"So when are you going to fire him?" I asked.

He paused before answering. "I'll do it tomorrow," he said.

Tomorrow's date would be May 7, 2007.

Finding the Murderer

On the morning of May 7, 2007, I kissed my husband goodbye and went to work…not knowing it would be the last time I would see him alive.

From that date through the early months of 2008, I spent a lot of time communicating with the investigating team assigned to Willie's case: Detective Rashid W. Sabur and Essex County Assistant Prosecutor Rachel Gran. I remember the many times my son-in-law, Hilery, and I had to go to the prosecutor's office or to the police station to meet with one or the other of them to discuss the case. The two investigators met with us on some occasions to report the status of the case and other times to ask questions that they thought might assist them in solving the murder. They were both helpful and comforting to us whenever we called or visited with them.

It was in the fall of 2007 that the investigating team told us that the handyman who worked for Willie was their prime suspect. It had been established that he was the last person to see Willie alive, and that he had attempted to pawn Willie's cell phone and use his credit cards at the Pathmark supermarket and the local Burger King restaurant. But they noted that because there were no witnesses to the crime, they were working on finding more-concrete evidence.

With that new information, my family and I were still very unhappy that a suspect had been identified but was still walking the streets with the potential to hurt other innocent people. This went on for at least nine months. Also, various people told my family members and me that on several occasions, the suspect had been seen out in public as if he had done nothing wrong.

One day early in 2008, I was singing in the choir—I remember it well because it was First Sunday, which is the Senior Choir's day to sing. Newark Mayor Cory Booker visited the Abyssinian Baptist Church. Of course, whenever dignitaries visit, they are invited to say a few words at the podium. It was about midway through the service that Mayor Booker addressed the congregation. He talked about the crime wave in Newark and what he and his constituency were doing to address it.

As I listened to the mayor speaking, I had a sort of epiphany. I knew he was familiar with Willie's case, because his comments about Willie's murder and two others the same week had been published in the newspapers. I felt as if I had been given a deeper insight from a divine power, and it manifested itself within me. I immediately decided that I would talk to Mayor Booker before he left the church even if I had to blow my trumpet as if I were one of Joshua's Israelites (Joshua 6:1-27). I was truly determined, and I was receiving a clear vision for a new perspective to find justice for Willie. I decided I would prepare myself to charge down the left aisle of the church as soon as the mayor finished speaking and he and his team began to leave the church. I felt he was my catalyst to get Willie's murderer arrested. Just as I predicted, there was applause as soon as Mayor Booker finished speaking, after which he and his entourage headed for the church exit. I immediately made a beeline for the exit, just as I had planned.

I caught up with the mayor in the church vestibule and tapped him on the shoulder. I told him I'd heard what he had just said about the high crime rate in Newark. "But what I want to know is, when are you going to arrest the man who killed my husband?" Introducing myself as Willie's wife, I reminded him about Willie's murder and his comments about it in the newspapers.

Mayor Booker looked startled, and he was speechless for a few moments before he responded. He talked to me for a few minutes and asked me a few questions. His manner was very sympathetic, cordial, and kind. He promised me he'd look into the situation and get back to me. I thanked him and shook his hand, and he was on his way. I returned to the choir, feeling good about what I had done and about the mayor's response.

Mayor Booker did exactly as he had promised. He called me a few days later and told me that he had reviewed the case and that his people were working on some additional details of it. On Friday, March 14—just a few weeks later—Al-Rashad Benbow was picked up and charged with murder, felony murder, and robbery.

Suspect is held in killing of deacon

Handyman accused in bludgeoning case

Essex County authorities said yesterday they had solved a murder that last year caused Newark Mayor Cory Booker to express anguish over the city's violent crime rate.

Al-Rashid Benbow, 33, is scheduled to be arraigned tomorrow for the May 2007 killing of Willie R. Taylor, an accountant and church deacon who was found bludgeoned to death in the basement of a home he owned and was renovating on Tillinghast Street in Newark, the Essex County Prosecutor's Office said.

A handyman, Benbow was arrested Friday and has been held in the Essex County Jail in Newark on $500,000 bail.

Investigators were led to Benbow after he used Taylor's credit cards to buy items from a Pathmark and Burger King and tried to sell the victim's cell phone after the slaying, according to the prosecutor's office.

Benbow, who lives in Newark, was charged with murder, felony murder and robbery.

Police say Benbow worked for Taylor and was the last person to see him alive on May 7, 2007, the day before his body was discovered. Earlier in the day, Taylor had been collecting rent from tenants at a home he owned in Irvington.

Detectives found Taylor's body just after 2 p.m. on May 8, and it was later determined he died of blunt force trauma to the head. They were called to the dwelling by Taylor's wife, Ella, and his son-in-law, after Taylor failed to return home. Also missing in the apparent robbery were Taylor's laptop computer, a checkbook, $2,200 in rent he had collected and his Jeep Cherokee.

Taylor, 67, grew up in Newark but had lived in Hillsborough for many years with his wife.

He was a deacon at the Abyssinian Baptist Church on West Kinney Street in Newark and often visited the sick on behalf of the congregation and served as a spiritual adviser to its ministers. The Rev. Perry Simmons described Taylor as his "right-hand man."

At a police graduation ceremony at City Hall two days after Taylor's death, Booker said a rash of murders in Newark - three in one week - had left him "twisted up." At one point, he compared the war in Iraq to the fight against crime in Newark.

"We have a war here in Newark," Booker said, slamming his fist into the podium as he gave his speech. "We have our challenges here. We have our fight right here."

Taylor's death was particularly upsetting, Booker said, because Taylor had been the victim of a "slaughter."

Booker declined comment yesterday.

By Guy Sterling
March 18, 2008
From *The Star-Ledger*

The Arraignment

Shortly after Benbow's arrest, during a Sunday-morning church service, I stood before my church's congregation and updated them on the status of Willie's murder case, including the upcoming court date. There was an overwhelming response to the news, and many church members wanted to attend. So, provisions were made for the church van to transport them to the arraignment on March 19, 2008. A large number of them accompanied me to the court. They told me they loved Deacon Taylor and wanted to be there for him and to support my family and me.

As a member of the Abyssinian Baptist Church Deacon Team, Deacon James Destin was Willie's communion partner. Among other services, the ABC Deacon Team provided communion to the sick and shut-in on communion Sunday. Deacon Destin was asked to be the spokesperson for the church group, and he was kind enough to accept the challenge.

At the arraignment, the defense and prosecuting attorneys had agreed on a plea bargain of 22 years. When Superior Court Judge Peter J. Vazquez asked Benbow to tell the court his version of what happened between him and Willie that day, Benbow stated that he had blacked out and didn't remember.

I listened intently as my husband's murderer testified in court.

As Benbow testified, I sat with the many church members who had come to support me. I sat with my elbows on my knees and listened attentively, staring directly at him. I wanted to hear exactly what he would say about why he killed Willie. Suddenly, a mysterious feeling came over me—a feeling that penetrated my spirit. A cloudlike film covered Benbow, and I began to feel total peace within my spirit. I knew at that moment that I felt no animosity toward this man for killing my husband. I know God changed my heart in that split second. I believe he did it for my health and well-being. I now know that what Benbow did to Willie is strictly between him and God. I no longer have any negative feelings toward him. What a blessing it has been to me!

Near the end of the arraignment, the judge allowed Deacon James Destin to address the court on behalf of me, my family, and our church members.

Deacon Destin told the court that as Christians, we must forgive Al-Rashad Benbow for murdering Deacon Taylor.

"We only hope that one day he will find it in his heart to repent for this horrible sin he has committed," he continued. "I've been married for thirteen years, and I can't imagine what it would be like to lose my spouse this way. Al-Rashad Benbow will get out of prison in 22 years and can start his life again, but Deaconess Ella Taylor will not be able to start again with Willie. She will never see her husband again."

Deacon Destin talked about the kind of person Willie was and how the church members loved him for his helpful and friendly manner, his service to the church, and his service to the Newark community. He also spoke of Willie's financial support and commitment to the ABC. He vividly expressed to the court the negative impact that the terrible tragedy had inflicted on Deacon Taylor's own family and church family.

◆

My entire family had the same reaction to Benbow's sentence. All of us felt strongly that he was a menace to society and that he should be imprisoned for life without the possibility of parole. The sentence of 22 years seemed like a reasonable plea bargain, but we wanted him to have a lifetime to think about what he did to such a good Christian man who did everything in his power to help him. We didn't feel the defendant should ever be allowed to walk the street again or have the opportunity to do such a horrific thing to another human being.

Newark handyman pleads guilty to fatally beating boss

NEWARK — A city man pleaded guilty to beating to death a 64-year-old man who had hired him as a handyman, authorities said. Rashad Benbow, 33, entered his plea to aggravated manslaughter and theft to state Superior Court Judge Peter Vazquez on Thursday, said Paul Loriquet, Essex County Prosecutor's Office spokesman.

Prosecutors have recommended that Benbow be sentenced to 22 years in prison for the 2007 death of Willie R. Taylor, a Hillsborough man who had employed Benbow to work at a Newark house he was remodeling. Benbow is scheduled to be sentenced on July 15.

Assistant Essex County Prosecutor Rachel Gran said that Taylor was a tax accountant who owned a number of Newark and Irvington properties he was renovating for resale. Taylor's wife, Ella, had asked him to hire Benbow after she had met his wife, Sandra Robinson Benbow, who was working as a temporary employee at University Medicine and Dentistry of New Jersey in Newark.

Ella Taylor said she is a computer programmer at the school, and that Benbow's wife mentioned he was looking for work.

Taylor hired Benbow to do odd jobs at 86 Tillinghast St., but later suspected the new employee was stealing tools and materials from the property, Gran said.

When Taylor confronted Benbow on May 7, 2007, he was severely beaten, Gran said.

Ella Taylor said she and her son-in-law found Taylor pummeled in the basement of the home at about 1:30 p.m. the next day. The medical examiner's said the cause of Taylor's death—blunt force trauma—understated what had happened to her husband.

"He literally broke his face," Taylor said.

Within hours of the crime, Benbow was recorded on video using Taylor's credit card at a Pathmark supermarket on Lyons Avenue in Newark, Gran said.

The next day, Benbow used it at a Burger King restaurant. He had also tried to sell Taylor's cell phone at Kinney's Electronics on Broad Street, and he stole Taylor's red Jeep, which was found in East Orange, Gran said.

Ella Taylor said she had mixed feelings about the plea agreement. After talking with prosecutors, family and her pastor, she decided that a 22-year prison sentence was preferable to risking Benbow's acquittal at a trial.

"I have peace about it," Taylor said. "No matter what we do, it won't bring Willie back."

By Paul Brubaker
June 29, 2009
From NJ.com; available at:
https://www.nj.com/news/2009/06/newark_handyman_pleads_guilty.html

The Appeal

Benbow appealed the decision, and his hearing was held on September 24 of the following year. His defense attorney argued five points that he claimed supported reversal of the conviction, but the court determined that there was no evidence that the crime was justified—even if, as the defendant claimed, Willie had pushed him when he demanded that Benbow leave the premises. The transcript of the appeal hearing follows.

STATE OF NEW JERSEY v. RASHAD BENBOW
Superior Court of New Jersey, Appellate Division.
STATE OF NEW JERSEY, Plaintiff–Respondent, v. RASHAD BENBOW, Defendant–Appellant.
DOCKET NO. A–5714–11T4
Decided: September 24, 2013

Before Judges Alvarez and Maven. Joseph E. Krakora, Public Defender, attorney for appellant (Alan I. Smith, Designated Counsel, on the brief). Carolyn A. Murray, Acting Essex County Prosecutor, attorney for respondent (John E. Anderson, Special Deputy Attorney General/ Acting Assistant Prosecutor, on the brief).

Defendant Rashad Benbow appeals the March 22, 2012 Law Division order denying his petition for post-conviction relief (PCR). We affirm.

Defendant entered pleas of guilty pursuant to an agreement with the State resolving an indictment that charged him with first-degree murder, N.J.S.A. 2C:11–3(a)(1), (2) (count one); first-degree felony murder, N.J.S.A. 2C:11–3(a)(3) (count two); first-degree robbery, N.J.S.A. 2C:15–1 (count three); and second-degree aggravated assault, N.J.S.A. 2C:12–1(b) (count four). He entered a guilty plea to an amended charge of first-degree aggravated manslaughter, N.J.S.A. 2C:11–4(a)(1), (c) (count one) and an amended count three, third-degree theft, N.J.S.A. 2C:20–2(b)(2)(d). On the aggravated manslaughter, the State agreed to recommend the imposition of a custodial term not to exceed twenty-two years subject to eighty-five percent parole ineligibility pursuant to the No Early Release Act (NERA), N.J.S.A. 2C:43–7.2(a). Additionally, the maximum sentence that could be imposed on the theft count was five years concurrent.

When defendant established his factual basis, the following exchange took place:

THE COURT: You understand that under the No Early Release Act you're not eligible for parole until you've completed 85 percent of your sentence? And under the plea recommendation in this case of 22 years, 85 percent—and this is an approximate number only—would be 18 years, eight months, and 15 days?

THE DEFENDANT: Yes, sir.

THE COURT: Other than what has been discussed with regard to your recommended—additionally, under the No Early Release Act, when you are released from custody you'll be on parole for a period of five years. And should you violate that parole, they could send you back to State prison for an unexpired period of the five years, even if it exceeded your original sentence; do you understand that?

THE DEFENDANT: Yes, I do.

Defendant completed the requisite "Supplemental Plea Form for No Early Release Act (NERA) Cases," which explained that he would be required to serve eighty-five percent of his sentence, and serve a five-year term of parole supervision upon his release.

In conformity with the agreement, defendant was sentenced to twenty-two years, subject to NERA, and a concurrent five years. Defendant's sentence was affirmed by the excessive sentence panel. See R. 2:9–11. At oral argument before the excessive sentence panel, counsel contended that the prosecutor's reference, during defendant's sentence hearing, to the fact that defendant took the victim's phone was unduly prejudicial and should not have been "singled out" in support of an aggravating factor. He also contended that the reference in defendant's "Uniform Defendant Intake" report to defendant's drug and mental health history should have warranted a finding by the court that mitigating factor four, substantial grounds tending to excuse or justify conduct, N.J.S.A. 2C:44–1(b)(4), applied. He also argued that the trial judge's failure to address mitigating factor five, that the victim "induced or facilitated" the crime, N.J.S.A. 2C:44–1(b)(5), was prejudicial error in the sentencing calculus.

Briefly summarized, defendant's charges arose from his killing of a sixty-eight-year-old victim, Willie Taylor. Taylor employed defendant as a handyman, and on May 7, 2007, told him "I don't have to keep hiring you. You're messing up, and you can't do none of the stuff I want you to do." When defendant threatened the victim, Taylor told him to "get out," and defendant responded "make me." Taylor pushed defendant, who slipped and fell. Defendant then repeatedly struck Taylor in the head and body, inflicting mortal wounds, leaving Taylor unconscious and bleeding. Defendant drove away in Taylor's Jeep, taking his credit card, which he used at a Pathmark and a Burger King, and his cell phone, which he unsuccessfully tried to sell.

At the sentencing hearing on September 15, 2009, defense counsel did not raise any mitigating factors. The sentencing judge found aggravating factors three, the risk defendant would reoffend, N.J.S.A. 2C:44–1(a)(3); six, the extent of his prior criminal history, N.J.S.A. 2C:44–1(a)(6); nine, the need to deter, N.J.S.A. 2C:44–1(a)(9); and twelve, that defendant inflicted harm on a victim of advanced age, N.J.S.A. 2C:44–1(a)(12); he found no mitigating factors. The judge observed that defendant had ten complaints filed against him as a juvenile, resulting in three adjudications, and fourteen arrests as an adult. This offense was his third indictable conviction. At the time the homicide occurred, defendant was thirty-two years old.

PCR counsel, in addition to renewing the arguments made during the excessive sentence presentation, also argued that trial counsel had not adequately explained to defendant the NERA consequences of the agreement. Further, counsel argued that the explanation made by the judge who accepted defendant's guilty plea did not correct the inadequate representation; specifically, defendant now claimed that, had he understood that he would not be eligible for parole until he served eighty-five percent of his time, he would not have entered a guilty plea.

The PCR judge denied the petition, concluding that the record demonstrated, from both defendant's plea form, as well as the courtroom colloquy, that, when the plea was entered, defendant understood the full ramifications of a NERA sentence. The judge also found that, although defendant may have believed that trial counsel would be arguing for fewer years of imprisonment at the time of sentencing, he had agreed to the sentence that was imposed. Defendant, therefore, failed to establish either prong of the Strickland[1] test. The court also stated that the record did not support the award of any mitigating factors. Therefore even if counsel was ineffective for failing to argue mitigating factors, there was no prejudice, as had such arguments been made they would have failed. Additionally, the court relied upon Rule 3:22–4, which bars any argument in support of PCR previously ruled upon, such as defendant's claims regarding mitigating factors, which had been addressed on appeal.

The court noted that, although in his pro se brief defendant asserted that his trial attorney did not investigate the case or rely on his statements, he did not identify facts that would have been revealed by additional investigation. Thus that claim was rejected. Since defendant had not made out a prima facie case for relief, defendant was not granted an evidentiary hearing.

On appeal, defendant argues:

POINT I

THE ORDER DENYING POST–CONVICTION RELIEF SHOULD BE REVERSED AND THE MATTER REMANDED FOR RESENTENCING BECAUSE THE DEFENDANT MADE A PRIMA FACIE SHOWING THAT HIS FOURTEENTH AMENDMENT DUE PROCESS RIGHT UNDER THE CODE OF CRIMINAL JUSTICE TO A SENTENCING HEARING IN WHICH ALL APPLICABLE MITIGATING FACTORS ARE DELINEATED WAS VIOLATED.

POINT II

THE ORDER DENYING POST–CONVICTION RELIEF SHOULD BE REVERSED BECAUSE DEFENDANT ESTABLISHED BY THE PREPONDERANCE OF THE EVIDENCE INEFFECTIVE ASSISTANCE OF TRIAL COUNSEL AT SENTENCING.

POINT III

THE COURT'S RULING DENYING POST–CONVICTION RELIEF VIOLATED THE DEFENDANT'S RIGHT TO EFFECTIVE ASSISTANCE OF COUNSEL AS GUARANTEED BY THE SIXTH AMENDMENT TO THE UNITED STATES CONSTITUTION.

POINT IV

THE PCR COURT MISAPPLIED ITS DISCRETION IN APPLYING THE PROCEDURAL BAR OF R. 3:22–5.

POINT V

DEFENDANT REASSERTS ALL OTHER ISSUES RAISED IN POST–CONVICTION RELIEF

(A)

TRIAL COUNSEL WAS INEFFECTIVE IN FAILING TO ADEQUATELY EXPLAIN TO THE DEFENDANT THE NERA CONSEQUENCES OF HIS PLEA.

We find no merit to these arguments. R. 2:11–3(e)(2). In this case, the record simply does not support any of defendant's contentions of error.

To the contrary, the record establishes that when the plea was entered, defendant was fully advised of the NERA consequences. The record does not include facts that would support any mitigating factors, evidenced by defendant's own statements, when he entered his guilty plea, that the victim's conduct neither excused nor justified the commission of the crime. Taylor's demand that defendant leave his home, even if accompanied by a push, was made after defendant threatened him. Similarly, defendant's statements to the probation officer who prepared the presentence report that he had abused drugs and had a mental health history alone were not sufficient to establish any mitigating factor.

Furthermore, the PCR court adequately considered defendant's pro se arguments. We too are satisfied that they lack merit, and, in fact, lack sufficient merit to warrant discussion in a written opinion. R. 2:11–3(e)(2).

Affirmed.

FOOTNOTES
FN1.Strickland v. Washington, 466 U.S. 668, 104 S.Ct. 2052, 80 L. Ed.2d 674 (1984).. FN1.Strickland v. Washington, 466 U.S. 668, 104 S.Ct. 2052, 80 L. Ed.2d 674 (1984).
PER CURIAM
Available at:
https://caselaw.findlaw.com/nj-superior-court-appellate-division/1644877.html

Taking the First Step

Once Al-Rashad Benbow started serving his 22-year prison sentence, Willie's family and mine turned our focus to the next question: "Where do we go from here?"

In considering that question, I began to take an intense look at my life and focus on just how much it had changed. That forced me to take a deep look inside my soul. I began to realize that I was much like a shipwreck, and I wasn't sure what to do with the remains. I didn't know how to get myself moving forward—I felt stuck. I felt like my world had disintegrated. Willie's murder is still the worst thing that has happened to me in my entire life.

The many months that followed Willie's murder was like living a distressing nightmare or one of those overwhelming crime movies. It was an extremely turbulent time for me. Willie's murder left both his family and mine devastated. The pain and grief were often unbearable. I felt like a zombie wandering the earth, not living…just existing. I had vivid flashbacks of Willie lying in a pool of blood on that concrete floor, his face mutilated like a thrown-away piece of garbage.

The hardest part of my new life without Willie was the first year or two after his death. I spent a lot of time alone. Hilery felt it wasn't safe for me to live alone in my home in Hillsborough at that time. He insisted that I live with him, Vanya, and their family in their home in Irvington, about 40 miles away. Hilery and Vanya said I'd be more stable there, and I conceded.

I realized that I needed to seek counsel from God. I prayed and asked God to help me endure, and the flashbacks slowly began to come less frequently. My family and I always wanted justice for my husband's murder, and our pain did diminish to some degree once Willie's murderer was in prison. We still feel the hurt sometimes, but God continues to help us heal.

Life Without Willie

My husband and I had lived together—just the two of us—for 23 years. Now I live alone. I have no one to cut my grass, no one to put gas in my car, no one to complete repairs around the house, no one to drive me to work on days when I don't feel up to making the 70-minute drive to Newark from Hillsborough. I have no one to drive me to church and can no longer look proudly at my husband as he performs his deacon duties at church—serving the congregation bread and wine, leading the church in prayer, and fellowshipping with the saints. I no longer have the honor of having him walk into our home, greet me with a kiss, and say, "Hi, Honey! How was your day?" Now I sleep alone. We traveled the world together, but now I have no traveling partner. And if I decide to travel, I don't have my husband to handle my luggage. I'm no longer able to enjoy going out to fancy restaurants to enjoy dinner and good conversation with my husband. I no longer get phone calls from him during the course of any given day and hear him ask, "How's your day going, Honey?" I still miss him so much, and my life will never be the same because of the horrific thing Benbow did to him.

Our children, grandchildren, sisters, brothers, nieces, and nephews still suffer also. They often speak of how they miss him and wish he could be with them. Some of them tell me he visits them in their dreams or visions. He was a very strong figurehead in our family. He was a confidant and family counselor to our sons-in-law and nephews. He was a teacher, counselor, advisor and friend to our daughters, goddaughter, and nieces. He was a solid rock to all of us. He was my friend, companion, lover, and business partner.

God Is in Control of Everything

I confess that for many months after my husband was murdered, I didn't know which way to turn. Little did I know that amidst the trauma, God was creating a newness in me. But at the center of that newness was confusion.

One night while I was having one of my moments seeing my dead husband on that concrete floor with his face bashed in, I asked God, "Where were you when that man was killing my husband?" God answered me as clear as water: "I was there," he said. I was surprised at God's answer—but I shouldn't have been. The interesting thing is that after God spoke into my spirit that night, I felt an inexplicable peace. It was the kind of peace I would feel when I saw a body of seawater calmly rolling with waves or when I would see the new blossoms on trees in the spring or when, as a child, I would hear a robin sing outside my mother's kitchen window. With that newfound peace, I felt no further need to question God about His presence during Willie's murder.

In my spirit, I was reminded that He is God. And if God was there and allowed Al-Rashad Benbow to kill my husband, then Willie must have reached his appointed time to go home and be with our Lord. All my life, I'd been taught as a Christian that God is love, God is everywhere, God is everything, God knows everything, God controls everything, God works for the highest good of all, and God can stop or start anything. Since God revealed to me that He was there as a witness to Willie's murder and God cannot make a mistake, I immediately understood that whatever I need to know about what happened to my husband and why it happened will also be revealed to me in God's own time. Yes, I suddenly knew that in His own time, God would reveal to me why this horrible thing happened to my husband. My heart was then filled with acceptance.

A Newness in Me

During those early months after Willie's murder, there were so many things happening within me that I felt discombobulated. This was my crisis time. But as time passed, I realized I was in the midst of growing into a new me. I sometimes felt as if I didn't know who I was. I wasn't sure what it was, but I felt in my spirit that I needed to explore the possibility that God was opening me up for some opportunity to use me for His glory and to be a blessing to other people.

As a young girl, I was introduced to the concept that within every adversity lies the seed of an equivalent advantage. That's why I look for the good in every situation. So I knew that my only solution was to submit myself to God's will and to trust that He will lead the way and reveal to me whatever I need to know or do for my future. This was the newness in me that I was starting to feel.

I began to feel my faith grow deeper and to realize that faith would be the key to my new life. I again felt a need for that same truth I had felt in those early years as a young girl. That thing I felt way deep down inside of me. That thing I had always longed for and was still trying to recognize. But I took comfort in my faith in God, knowing that He was directing my life.

In my search for truth as a young person in my early years growing up, I had discovered that I was special. Through reading God's Word and attentively listening to messages delivered by the clergy, I have come to understand that God did, in fact, make me special and create me for His special purpose. And since God is in control, there is a divine reason for everything that happens to me. I started to understand that God was taking care of me as He always had and that He would carry me and direct my way until I can do it for myself. It reminded me of the poem "Footprints in the Sand," about the man who had a dream about walking along the beach with the Lord as scenes of his life flashed before him. The man saw that through most of the journey, there were two sets of footprints—one his own and one the Lord's—but only one set during the darkest times of his life. The man asked the Lord why He had abandoned him when he needed Him most, and the Lord replied that when there was only one set of footprints, it was because He had carried the man during those difficult times. In the same way, God has continued to carry me. The poem revealed to me why I was experiencing a newness in me. God had done a "new thing" in me and put me on a trajectory for His plan for my life.

God's Plan for My Life

I could now clearly understand that I must trust God, obey God, and focus on God's will rather than on my crisis. As I made this change, my situation gradually shifted from crisis to healing. I sensed a change in me. I felt I was moving toward God's plan for my life.

From a young age, I was taught that God had a plan for my life. I would ask myself, "What is my purpose? Why am I here?" Along the way, I learned that God's predestined will is irresistible, unchangeable, and unconditional. *(I will instruct you and teach you in the way which you should go; I will guide you with My eye.* [Psalm 32:8)]

In integrating all of that information, I started to clearly see that the only path to God's plan for my life is to be led by God through Jesus Christ and The Holy Spirit (the Trinity). *(At that day you will know that I am in My Father, and you in Me, and I in you.* [John 14:20]) So, I reconciled myself to that truth.

Once I became an adult, I began to think that God's plan for my life involved vocations like documenting, teaching, or training. Over the years, I have continued to be drawn to professions that required skills relevant to areas like computer programmer, text processing manager, human resources analyst, teacher, and trainer. They all required proficiency in writing, documenting, or teaching. Since I didn't precisely plan my career path, I believe The Holy Spirit directed me through my past professions.

About ten years ago, I started feeling that I had absorbed such a variety of personal development information that I wanted to share it with the world somehow. That's what prompted me to consider writing a book.

Throughout my adult life, I've read self-help books and studied the Bible, metaphysical readings and teachings, and the Law of Attraction. There was a time when I would listen to The Secret on CD every morning before I went to work. It was my "fix" for the day. The Secret is a self-help book by Rhonda Byrne, based on the belief of the Law of Attraction that thoughts can change a person's life directly. *(For as he thinks in his heart, so is he.* [Proverbs 23:7])

In my spirit, I began to understand that God was giving me guidelines on how to live in this world. I got excited and wanted to tell everybody how easy it could be for them to make their life work. I wanted to yell it from the rooftops, if that were at all possible. At that moment, I had an epiphany: "Let go and let God." I began to see what God wanted my life's work to be: to share with the world a better way to live. And that better way is simply to ask, believe, and receive. But I didn't know how to share that concept with the world or even where to start. So, I decided to just "let go and let God," keeping in mind Jesus' words in the scripture: *Therefore I tell you, whatever you ask for in prayer, believe that you have received it, and it will be yours.* (Mark 11:24)

I then knew that God would provide a way for me to share my thoughts about the "added value" embedded in exploring the deeper meaning of that scripture.

That thinking evolved into conversations with God. I realized that my key role was obedience, so I promised Him that I would trust Him and that I would obey Him in our newfound relationship. In my spirit, I committed to the scripture: *Trust in the Lord with all your heart, and lean not on your own understanding. In all your ways acknowledge Him, and He shall direct your paths.* (Proverbs 3:5-6)

I promised myself within my spirit that whenever God spoke to my heart to perform an action, whether for me or someone else, I would obey His voice. I prayed for discernment to recognize His voice and the power to keep the enemy away from me. In my spirit, I decided to do whatever God commanded me to do, and I would do it with tenacity. In my spirit, I promised to volunteer to assist in areas where it was clear to me that God had gifted me with a talent to do a particular deed or thing. So, my focus on writing a book then became somewhat of an obsession, but I continued to let go and let God.

Since obedience to God was the key guideline for my life, I consulted with Him on almost everything. I would find myself talking out loud to Him as if He were there with me in the flesh. He became my closest companion. It reminded me of those years when I was a young girl and I thought my mother was crazy until I realized she was simply talking with God.

Therapy

Having committed to obeying God's voice, I sensed a deep feeling within my spirit that drew me to a book about the grieving process. A fellow church member—my sister friend Deaconess Dorothy Clark—had given me a book, and The Holy Spirit directed me to read it again. I felt an overwhelming need to figure out what stage of grief I was in and what progress I had made so far, if any. It was around June 2009, and Willie had been gone for two years.

Please understand that the following describes my personal journey in dealing with my husband's death; it isn't intended to represent how others process their own grief. After reading various sources on the subject, I came to understand that people grieve in different ways. Some people experience more than one stage at a time, while others regress to a previous stage.

As I continued to read the book Sister Dorothy had given me and understand the stages of grief, The Holy Spirit directed me to seek the help of a professional counselor. So I started my search for a therapist who could help me handle all these erratic feelings and emotions that I didn't know what to do with. My company's employee counseling department gave me a list of participating therapists in my health insurance plan, and I spoke with a few of them. Finally, through God's guidance, I was blessed to find Ms. Venita Harris Welcome, a counselor and coach based in Somerset. Ms. Welcome seemed to be the perfect person to help me. She remained my therapist for many months and helped me maintain some sense of sanity until I began to feel better.

I felt comforted to have a new resource to help me through my period of emptiness and despair. Ms. Welcome helped me first by teaching me how to remove my armor. As a trained professional, she knew the right words to allow me to express my true feelings. She elevated me to a state of total fearlessness by encouraging me to vocalize my deepest thoughts. She assured me that her profession required confidentiality, so I wasn't apprehensive about being completely open with her. At times, I was surprised at some of the things that came out of my mouth—surprised at some of the things I felt deep down inside of me.

I found that as a complement to my counseling sessions with Ms. Welcome, the five stages of grief turned out to be a very useful way to measure how I was progressing and what I could expect in moving forward. I started comparing the stages of grief to my feelings and behavior as a way to identify which stage I was in.

During my early sessions with Ms. Welcome, the visions of Willie dead on that concrete basement floor persisted. That suggested that I was in the first stage of grief: denial. I still hadn't accepted that Willie was gone forever and was never coming back.

With each session, I would get more insight into which stage I was in and how my healing was progressing. For example, one day I talked with her about my responsibility for attending to the affairs of Willie's Aunt Jennie. At the time, Aunt Jennie was 86 years old and in a nursing facility. She had no children, and her nieces and nephews weren't able to help her. It seemed I was the only one who could. It was like when we played a game of tag as a child someone got tagged: "Tag, you're it!" There were no other options.

As I continued to discuss Aunt Jennie and all the other things I was taking care of by myself, I realized I was really angry with Willie. I was in stage 2: anger. I was furious with him for dying, leaving everything that we had built together for me to manage all by myself. So many things were beginning to require my attention. I had to plan my life around accommodating my needs and Aunt Jennie's needs. I had to make sure she had the proper clothing and many other basic necessities. I had to pick her up from the nursing facility and take her to the Abyssinian Baptist Church with me on Sundays—she insisted on going to church, and I knew how much she loved it. On top of all that, I had to handle her business affairs. At times, it was overwhelming. I had to turn to God and ask for strength and courage to endure.

I seemed to have skipped the third stage of grief: bargaining. I'm certain the reason I didn't bargain with God is that my heart and my spirit would *never* allow me to even entertain the idea. From the time I was very young, my mother taught us children to always give the highest honor and respect to God and that I could pray to Him for what I want, but when I make a request, I should always end my prayer to God with "if it is your will." So to me, just the thought of negotiating with God is unacceptable and disrespectful. My thinking on the subject is confirmed in the Book of Genesis, which tells of people who bargained with God. In chapters 18:16-33, Abraham unsuccessfully bargains with God to save Sodom and Gomorrah; then, in chapter 28:20-22, Jacob bargains with God's messenger, who has attacked him.

As time passed, everything seemed to become jumbled and in disarray. I was very bewildered as I began to comprehend the true magnitude of my loss. My therapy sessions and the stages of grief had finally starting showing me that I would be alone—that my husband was gone and would never return. I became despondent, isolating myself in my safe haven—the room I stayed in at Vanya and Hilery's house. As I reflected on memories of things Willie and I did together, I felt a sense of emptiness and despair. All these were signs that I was in stage 4 of grief: depression.

Over the next few months, as I began to adjust to life without Willie, my life became a little calmer and more organized. My physical symptoms decreased, and I was less depressed. As I continued to pray and go to my therapy sessions with Ms. Welcome, I gradually improved. I started gaining momentum, and it seemed I was getting my flow of life back. I was in stage 5: acceptance.

At that point—about a year after I'd begun therapy—I told Ms. Welcome I felt I didn't need to attend therapy sessions with her any longer, and she agreed. So I stopped going to therapy but continued to monitor my progress and pray to God for guidance.

God really started to take over and reveal His power by showing me my healing. There's one scenario I remember very well because it came as a big surprise to me: Sister Stedman Ashe, leader of the Mission Circle at my church, asked me to be the keynote speaker for the Missionary Annual Day Service Celebration on June 27. I was shocked, but I shouldn't have been—mainly because I knew in my heart that God had blessed me with the ability to do it, and I had successfully facilitated many of the women's workshops at our church. Also, since I had promised to assist in areas where God had gifted me with a talent to do a particular thing and being a deaconess in the church, I felt an obligation to accept the request. Even so, I was still somewhat hesitant—but in my spirit, I know now that God made me say yes. I heard myself say it, but it seemed as if it just rolled out of my mouth as if it were coming from someone other than me. It became crystal clear to my heart that it came from God. It's something that has happened to me often—the words just rolled off my lips as if they were coming from someone else. In cases like those, I know the words are coming from my spiritual self.

As I continued to digest the idea, I realized it would be an honor to deliver a word from God to the congregation on such an occasion. I wasn't sure what I would speak about, but I had sufficient time to prepare. But God! God gave me my topic: "Understanding God's Purging Process." It took Him a little time to give it to me, but as soon as He did, I knew for sure it was the right topic for me during that time in my life.

While I was speaking to the congregation, God revealed to me that the purpose of sharing my story was to help me understand the status of my healing process in regard to the death of my husband. It was a cathartic experience for me, and I purged many things to help me accept Willie's death. Wow—that was so powerful! Power as only God can exhibit. When I was finally able to wrap my thoughts around the mystical thing God had done that day, I felt transformed by that phenomenon and in a state of renewal.

I also realized that I'd become more functional and that my mind had started to work more fluently again, which was evidenced by my delivery of my sermon to the congregation that day. As I further examined what God had given me to share with the congregation, I understood more clearly that God was helping me and would continue to help me find practical solutions to the problems in my life. I also came to understand that I could live my life without Willie, and I began to get excited about reconstructing myself and my life.

Some people may not understand why it may take someone a long time to heal. They may feel—and sometimes may even vocalize—that the person should "get over it" and rejoin the land of the living. Everybody responds to loss differently, so it's important not to pass judgment on someone who's going through the grieving process.

Living With the Family

I believe that when I was living with Hilery and Vanya, they noticed a change in me and were concerned. But they were more at ease once I told them I was undergoing therapy with Ms. Venita Welcome. Since I was transitioning into my new life with God, it may have appeared to them that I was somewhat withdrawn from reality.

When I was a young girl, my mother taught me that God could fix anything. So, being in such an uncertain, fragile, and lethargic state, I naturally turned to God. I didn't know what else to do. God had truly become my closest friend. He didn't walk beside me; he walked in front of me and protected me. I could feel His presence. *(Surely He shall deliver you from the snare of the fowler and from the perilous pestilence.* [Psalm 91:3]) Psalm 91 talks about the safety of abiding in the presence of God, and that's where I found my safety. The Bible teaches of Satan as the fowler who betrays unguarded souls. So I desperately needed protection from Satan, and I found my protection in God.

When we first agreed that I would live with Vanya and Hilery, Vanya suggested we buy a mother-daughter house. But I didn't want to give up my home in Hillsborough, so instead, we agreed that I would continue to stay with them for a while and go home on weekends to check on my house.

"Stay with us for a while," they said. Well, I lived with my daughter and her husband from June 2007 to June 2014—a total of seven years. It was a big surprise to them—and to me! I was stuck. I couldn't live alone. I didn't remember this at the time, but scholars believe that the number seven is the template for mankind. It's a number of completeness, divine perfection, or something that is finished, as in the creation week in Genesis 2:1-3. I found the connection interesting. Perhaps I needed seven years to complete my healing.

That seven-year period was my safety net—an escape into the denial that God gave me in order to grow me into the person he wanted me to be. Vanya had gladly volunteered to convert her in-home office into a private room for me. God knew I needed that safe haven —that room that I retreated to each day when I got home from work. My daughter and I went shopping to decorate it so that I would be comfortable during my stay. The room was beautiful, and I spent the majority of my free time in it. It became my sanctuary.

Even so, it was the hardest time of my new life, because sometimes I felt displaced, sometimes I felt numb, and sometimes I felt lost. But my family was there for me. They always tried to involve me in family activities and all the things families do.

Our family consisted of Vanya and Hilery; their son, Terrell, and daughters, Jha'na and Kayla; two cats, Toes and Fingers; and our dog, Milk. Terrell's high school classmate and best friend, Herby Augustin, was also a part of our family. He became very dear to me, like the son I never had. Herby has a heart of gold, and he became my sidekick. I feel he is one of the earth angels that God strategically planted in my life to help me. (More about earth angels later.) Herby did so much for me, like riding with me to Hillsborough every weekend and helping me with chores and errands. He even drew the illustrations for this book. To me, he has truly been a gift from God. Even now, if I need Herby for anything, he makes himself available to help me. And he knows I'm always there for him, too.

One weekend in 2013, after it had snowed about eight inches, I asked Herby to ride with me to my home in Hillsborough to shovel the snow. Of course, he said yes without hesitation. When we arrived, we were amazed at the amount of snow on my property. Some of the snowdrifts were up to my waist. Herby walked up my 100-foot-long driveway to get the shoveling equipment from the garage and told me to walk up my neighbor's driveway, which had already been shoveled. Then he made a path for me from my neighbor's driveway to my house. I did my best to step in his tracks, but I slipped and fell on my butt a few times. Herby was right there to help me. Even now, we still laugh about what a fiasco that day was with all that snow.

Since I had lived for the last 23 years with only one person, having so many different personalities in our house was a new experience for me. But being with my God-given family made me smile. I believe God creates a special bond within the family unit that brings out happiness. And that special bond brought out the happy part of me. I especially enjoyed our game night and our dinners together. I also offered to cook for the family on Wednesdays. Everyone loved that. One time, Vanya and Hilery went on a nine-day getaway cruise, and I was in charge. I have a very good relationship with my grandchildren, but I didn't know what to expect with their parents gone. But we had a great time, and the days and nights rolled along without incident.

A good thing about the new life of mine was that my job was ten minutes away and my church, fifteen. My travel time was cut by nearly two hours a day, so that part of my life was much better for me.

To sum up my new life, it consisted mainly of going to work daily and going to church on Tuesday nights for Bible study; on Thursday nights for choir rehearsal; and on Sundays for Sunday school, preaching, and fellowshipping with the saints. I spent most of the balance of my time in my room—my safe haven. Plus, Herby and I always went to my home in Hillsborough on the weekends for a day or two to check on things.

Because I was the only person up and about at 5:30 in the morning, our cat Toes decided I would be the one to feed him. I resisted at first, but he relentlessly followed me around, coming into my room and doing whatever he could do to get my attention until I would feed him just to get rid of him. I got used to it after a while, and feeding Toes became part of my morning ritual. Ultimately, Toes and I became friends and he began to behave as if he appreciated me for taking care of him.

My Best Friend

I consistently tried hard to embrace my new life, but living without my earthly best friend, Willie, was a challenge. Remember, he had been my best friend for 23 years—a best friend that I could see, touch, and smell.

But with my new life came my *new* Best Friend—someone I can't see, touch, or smell. But I can feel His presence, and I can hear Him talking to me. Of course, that Best Friend is God—God through Jesus Christ and The Holy Spirit.

It's been some time now since I realized I would be physically alone after Willie's death. But it was never a surprise to God. He had me covered. As a Christian, I was always taught I could be sure that God would always be My Best Friend and would never leave me or forsake me. I have found this to be true because He has always been there for me and with me. Over the years, He has done amazing work in my life. I'm reminded that God is always with me by way of The Holy Spirit, who resides inside of me…and inside of us all. *(Even the Spirit of truth, whom the world cannot receive, because it neither sees Him nor knows Him; but you know Him, for He dwells with you and will be in you.* [John 14:17])

Through study, I learned that my spirit is that part of my being thought of as the center of life. Having accepted the Lord Jesus Christ as my Savior, my spirit is sealed, and my sin does not enter into my spirit. *(You were sealed with The Holy Spirit of promise.* [Ephesians 1:13]) That tells me my spirit remains righteous and holy. It is pure and uncontaminated. The born-again part of me is as holy as Jesus.

I learned that my spirit and my soul work together with my heart. My spirit is always open to God because it is that part of me that connects my essence to The Holy Spirit of the Trinity (God, Jesus, and The Holy Spirit). The Bible defines The Holy Spirit as the Spirit of God, the divine source of all life, and a special manifestation of God's Divine Presence.

Through my life experiences, I have learned that my soul is not always open to God because it works in conjunction with my mind. My mind responds to what I taste, hear, smell, see, and feel (the physical aspect). Then when I allow emotions to dominate me, my soul and body work against my spirit, impeding the flow of the power of God on the inside of me. Therefore, I pray that I continue to improve upon focusing on keeping my mind, soul, and spirit in agreement so I can experience the supernatural things of God flowing through me, through my life, and to others. "Supernatural things of God" refers to those times when God provides solutions to a complex problem I may be having. Other times, it's when I misplace something and I ask God to show me where it is. In those cases, I always find it because of my strong belief that I will. *(Therefore I say to you, whatever things you ask when you pray, believe that you receive them, and you will have them.* [Mark 11:24])

Another type of supernatural occurrence with God that I've experienced is "assignments"—when I take on tasks without realizing I'm committing to them. They seem to come from my spirit, not directly from me. One such incident happened in 2010, which I'll explain further in Lesson 7. I was talking on the phone with my daughter Debbie about problems she was having with her landlord. She told me that she needed to move out of her home and find a new place to live on short notice but that it'd take several years of saving before she'd be able to buy her first home. When Debbie broke into tears, I heard myself telling her I'd buy her a home. To this day, it feels as if my response to her did not come from me—I can't explain it. But it was clear to me that God had made me offer to buy my daughter a home, so of course I did it.

These life experiences have enhanced my understanding of the connection between the spirit within me and The Holy Spirit, and they have confirmed for me that my spirit is that part of me that connects me to The Holy Spirit of God, the divine source of all life. I now see that to be led by God, I must maintain daily communication with Him through prayer, hearing His voice through The Holy Spirit and through His word (the Holy Bible), and then I must be obedient to His guidance (what he directs me to do).

And since the death of my husband, I have felt a newness about how I see God's role in my life. So I've claimed God as My Best Friend, and I talk with him more frequently for praise, thanks, and guidance. I have gained a peace within myself by doing that, because now I know that God, through Jesus Christ and The Holy Spirit, is in my driver's seat. *(Be anxious for nothing, but in everything by prayer and supplication, with thanksgiving, let your requests be made known to God.* [Philippians 4:6-7])

As gospel singer Marvin Sapp says, I "Never Would Have Made It" through that whole grieving process without the guidance of The Holy Spirit. My evolving path has truly been led by God through Jesus Christ and The Holy Spirit. He put people around me and in my path to help me, or he would lead me to read or hear something to make me notice what He was doing or wanted me to do. I surrendered myself to His lead, and He continues to show me His will for my life.

I feel that God wants me to show the world, through this book, how He has walked with me through trust and obedience, leading me to His plan for my life. *(When you pass through the waters, I will be with you; And through the rivers, they shall not overflow you. When you walk through the fire, you shall not be burned, nor shall the flame scorch you.* [Isaiah 43:2])

Part 3

My New Life

Who Am I Now?

As I fumbled blindly through the maze of my new life, I learned many life lessons. Fortunately, I had My Best Friend with me to guide and direct me. That gave me the courage to keep trying and to keep moving forward to find my place in the world again. And although living with my family enriched my spirit, I knew I needed more.

That thirst for more incited me to examine a series of recent events. I call these observations "life lessons" because they took me to another level as a human being. I began to examine myself and what I was doing with my life. I wanted to make sure I was aligned with God's plan for my life. To try to figure it out, I started a more frequent dialog with My Best Friend through prayer. He provided solutions through His word (the Bible) and by speaking to my heart.

The solution He provided to me was to do a detailed mental examination of my feelings, thoughts, and emotions. The results were interesting and informative.

For much of my life, my work had defined my being; it had become my identity. When I was young, people would ask me what I wanted to do when I grew up. As I grew older, people would ask me what my educational discipline and career goals were. Once I became a part of corporate America, I was often asked, "What do you do?"

These things had previously shaped my soul to the extent that I saw myself primarily as a worker. What I did for a living defined who I was. Who I was as a person was defined by my vocation. My identity had become what I did for a living.

When I took my blinders off and began to look inside myself, I had another epiphany. There was a shift in my thinking, and I started to look at how I should be, think, and act. I realized that, as a Christian, my core identity is determined not by what I do for a living, but by my relationship with God through Jesus Christ and His plan for my life.

As my way of thinking changed, everything else in my life also changed. Work—whether paid or unpaid—continued to matter, but mainly as a way of offering myself in service to God and then to the world as His representative. I started to feel that I must give back to the universe more than I take and I must always listen for direction from The Holy Spirit as to who or what I needed to focus on.

It was during that time in my life that I truly began to recognize My Best Friend's voice. I simply knew without question when He spoke to me. I knew when He provided me with a specific directive, and I knew when He removed some obstacle from my path. We must always remember that God provides His guidance and directives through His word and by speaking to our spirit and our heart. It is critical that we never forget to listen for God's guidance.

My decisions about how to invest my time, my money, and my kindness are guided by my truth and eternal values rather than by how they can enhance my professional success. Most of all, my core sense of being depends not on how successful I am with what I do, but on the undeniable and unchangeable fact that I am beloved by God; I belong to God; and He is my Lord, Savior, and Best Friend. He will never leave me, nor will He ever forsake me.

By completing the task My Best Friend had provided, I realized that my eyes had been opened and I could see. I had a déjà vu moment and reflected on the cataract surgery I'd had in the year 2014. After the surgery, my doctor told me my eyesight had improved 100 percent. My eyes functioned like new, and I felt like I was seeing the world for the first time. Everything looked so clear and brand new. It was a hallelujah moment.

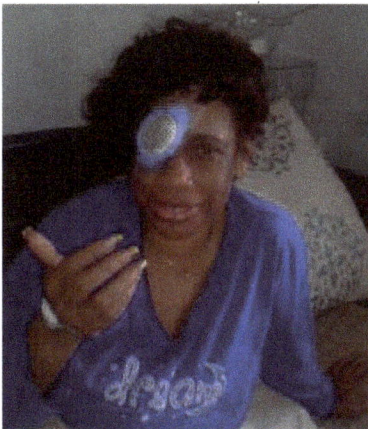

I recuperated from cataract surgery in 2014.

My newfound perspective was also a hallelujah moment. I began to examine myself as a person. In doing so, I realized that my life lessons had enhanced me as a person; I had become a better human being because of them. I felt like I was ten feet tall, healthy, wealthy, wise, and beautiful. I felt like somebody important, with so much to share.

The stimulus was like an electrical impulse. It gave me the incentive, enthusiasm, and excitement I needed to write this book. By sharing my life lessons, I want to give my readers a tool for self-improvement and catapult them toward a path that will benefit their way of life. I want to provide guidance that will help them lead fuller, more comfortable, enhanced lives.

I believe God wants me to support and encourage my readers. I believe He wants me to show the world that my life is a testimony on how to overcome grief and establish true intimacy with God—proof that ultimately, with God, we will reach our full potential and invoke the plan He has for us by connecting with our universal power and implementing our universal good.

> God will help us overcome any obstacle life throws in our path.
> God has no telephone,
> but I talk to Him.
> He has no Facebook,
> but He is my Friend.
> He has no Twitter,
> but I follow Him.
> God is My Life!

Life Lessons

As I reflect on my life—especially what I've been through since the murder of my husband—I realize how much I've learned from my experiences. These are 15 of my most valuable life lessons.

Lesson #1: God is: (2007)

I've been taught about God all my life. I was reared as a Baptist Christian, and my mother had an intimate relationship with Our Lord. I originally learned by watching her.

Being taught that "God is" and actually learning that "God is" are two different scenarios. Teaching is the presentation of ideas or principles by someone else, generally an authority; it involves a teacher and a student (learner). Learning is the acquisition of knowledge or skills; it can be taught or it can be obtained through experience or self-study.

Ever since my husband was murdered, I have learned that to survive, I must surrender my future to God—simply because I don't know what to do with myself and God has been my only trustworthy resource.

I learned that "God is"! God is love. God is everywhere. God is everything. God is the universal mind. And because He can't tell a lie, He will do everything He promises. Sometimes He will see our heart and simply grant our desire. *(Delight yourself also in the Lord, and He shall give you the desires of your heart.* [Psalms 37:4]) Other times, we must ask Him first. *(Ask, and it will be given to you; seek, and you will find; knock, and it will be opened to you.* [Matthew 7:7-8]) It all depends on the "who," "what," "why," "when," "where," and "how" of a situation that God will respond… and often there is a delay in His response because it may involve a solution that is for "the highest good of all." That's why it's critical to be careful about how we communicate our request to Him and we must be patient in waiting for His response. *(But those who wait on the Lord shall renew their strength; they shall mount up with wings like eagles, they shall run and not be weary, they shall walk and not faint.* [Isaiah 40:31])

As the saying goes, "When you get to the end of your rope, tie a knot in it and hold on"—a knot of trust, a knot of faith, and a knot of patience.

I believe we're all connected through The Holy Spirit and that whatever God lets happen is for the highest good of us all, even when we don't understand it. But there are invisible stipulations in our daily dealing with God: we must have strong faith in Him and trust in Him; we must be obedient to Him; we must have a forgiving spirit; and we must have patience. These behaviors are essential, but with them comes a peace that passes all understanding. *(Be anxious for nothing, but in everything by prayer and supplication, with thanksgiving, let your requests be made known to God; and the peace of God, which surpasses all understanding, will guard your hearts and minds through Christ Jesus.* [Philippians 4:6-7])

Lesson #2: In time of loss, trust Jesus. (2007)

I often felt that my family members were going to and fro, living their own lives, while I was left to fill my void as best I could by myself. I realized I had to trust Jesus for every detail of my setback if I wanted to reverse it into a comeback. So, I resorted to the only real help I knew.

I wanted joy to return to my life, so I prayed for that. The Holy Spirit directed me to unite with other people to help me refocus on getting my life back. I started to reach out to others for comfort, and I decided to be more social. So on May 14, with the help of the Newark-based newspaper *The Star-Ledger*, I created a permanent memorial page for Willie. The page provides a forum for Willie's family and friends to share words of encouragement and write to him if they choose to do so. The URL of the page is https://www.legacy.com/obituaries/name/willie-taylor-obituary?pid=88043412.

Since then, many people have written on Willie's memorial page. Using this vehicle, I have been able to create a permanent depository for messages to Willie and all his friends and family members. I also established a list of people I email every year on the anniversary of Willie's death, inviting them to leave an expression of comfort or comments to us.

As God would have it turn out, Willie's memorial page has been very comforting to me, and it has helped me recover from my grief. One example of a comment that has brought me comfort is the following message from my friend and co-worker Marcelle.

==

May 7, 2011

Dearest Ella:

Your strength continues to be an inspiration to me at all times, but most particularly in those times of strife and difficulty. I have no doubt at all that Wil is incredibly proud of you. During the time you and I worked together, the grace with which you handled every challenge God handed you never ceased to amaze me and in the end helped to teach me to be grateful not only for what I already have, but for what is coming, as well. I consider myself eternally grateful to count you among my friends. I will always love you.

Marcelle Costanza
Somerset, NJ

==

Lesson #3: Professional help can be valuable to the healing process. (2008-2009)

God had spoken into my spirit and directed me to seek the help of a professional counselor. After much research, I was fortunate to find Ms. Venita Harris Welcome from the Christian Wellness Center of New Jersey, who remained my therapist for about a year.

Ms. Welcome was a tremendous source of help to me during a time when I felt I had lost everything and was fearful of the future. She knew how to make me trust her so that I felt comfortable enough to express my true feelings and share my deepest thoughts. Getting my feelings out into the open helped me to better understand them and release the stress of embedded emotions. She helped me accept Willie's death so that I could begin to heal and move forward. I don't believe I would've been able to do it without her professional help.

Lesson #4: God will provide a solution to a critical problem. (2008-2009)

Willie and I had been married for 23 years and built a solid life together—a life of friendship, love, and companionship. We were involved in real estate, including a property belonging to his Aunt Jennie. Aunt Jennie's husband, Willie's Uncle Bud, had died in 2003, leaving Willie as her closest relative and caregiver. Willie was preparing her property for rental when he was murdered in 2007.

Willie and I had been very close to Aunt Jennie and Uncle Bud. They had no children and were like parents to us, even standing as parents in our wedding in 1984 since our parents were elderly and unable to travel to New Jersey.

Aunt Jennie had been in a nursing home since 2005. After Willie's death, I was the only person left to take care of her since her niece and nephew weren't able to help. So I made regular visits to the nursing home to see her and make sure she was being taken care of properly, picked her up and took her to church on Sundays, and managed her practical affairs, including her house and her finances. It was a tremendous burden, because I was still mourning the death of my husband, working a full-time job, and taking care of my own household.

The biggest problem with it was Aunt Jennie's house. I was able to take care of Aunt Jennie herself, but the situation with her house was much more intricate. Every time I saw her, she'd ask, "When can I go to my house? I want to go home." I knew I couldn't sell the house, because it meant too much to her. So the only option was to renovate it and rent it out. I clearly didn't know how to renovate a house. But I knew I had to do something, so I prayed about it and was directed to seek advice from my friends and acquaintances.

What happened next reminds me of the story in the Bible about Abraham and the ram in the bush: *Then Abraham lifted his eyes and looked, and there behind him was a ram caught in a thicket by its horns. So Abraham went and took the ram, and offered it up for a burnt offering instead of his son.* (Genesis 22:13) Rodney Sanders was my ram in the bush.

Rodney came to me through my goddaughter, Glynis Sanders, who is Rodney's sister. One day during our lunch break, I was telling her about my dilemma with Aunt Jennie's house and she told me, "Oh, my brother does that kind of work. I'll ask him if he can help you." Rodney turned out to be a tremendous help to me and was truly my ram in the bush. Within a six-month period, Rodney had gotten everything out of the house, completed all the necessary repairs, and found new tenants for both apartments.

Lesson #5: People care, and that helped me heal. (2010)

In the spring of 2010, my fun-loving friend Kara decided it would be a wonderful distraction for me to go to St. Thomas with her and her family. I had never been to St. Thomas before and was still grieving over the loss of my husband, so the idea was very appealing to me. Her husband, Darrell, invited his Aunt Mary to come along. Mary was close to my age, which made it even more enjoyable for me. So all of us, along with their 10-year-old daughter, Skyler, went to St. Thomas for ten days. As usual, Kara planned everything. We were all very excited about our trip.

What a great time we had. Our rooms were fabulous. Sometimes we spent time together and other times we each went our own way. But we enjoyed everything we did—early breakfast on the boardwalk, a winery, boat rides, a river cruise, the beach, a tour of the island, and lots of other fun things. We even bought food at the local food market and had dinner together several times. I'll never forget how kind Kara was to arrange such a beautiful diversion for me at a time when I so desperately needed it. A hallelujah is a good way to express how I feel about that trip and what it did for my healing: *Hallelujah!*

Lesson #6: God will provide a vehicle to promote my healing. (2010)

In late April of 2010, Sister Stedman Ashe, the leader of the Mission Circle at my church, asked me to be the keynote speaker at the church's Missionary Annual Day Service Celebration in June. I believe God provided me with the opportunity as a way for me to advance my healing and show my progress to the world. I knew for sure that I could do it with the help of My Best Friend. I had plenty of time to prepare—almost two months.

The sermon topic My Best Friend and I selected was "Understanding God's Purging Process." My message to the congregation was outstanding and very well received. At the end of the service, Pastor Simmons shook my hand and told me I had done a fine job of exegeting the text. It made me happy to get his stamp of approval.

I was proud of how well my sermon went, and I felt more alive than I had felt in a very long time. The experience confirmed for me that My Best Friend would always help me find realistic solutions to any problems I might face as I move forward on my journey without Willie. I was optimistic about rebuilding my life. Sometimes I listen to my sermon over and over again to remind myself of the progress I've made.

I presented my sermon at the Missionary Annual Day Service Celebration on June 27, 2010.

A CD of my sermon, titled "Understanding God's Purging Process."

The ABC Mission Group on the day I presented my sermon (left to right): the late Evangelist Christine Smith, Rev. Ileathern McLeod, me, Sister Stedman Ashe, and Sister Dorothy Harris.

Lesson #7: God is able to speak through me and use me for His purpose when I have an open heart. (2010-2011)

My daughter Debbie normally calls me every day to talk about what's going on in her life. I appreciate it, because she lives about 400 miles away. Our daily chats help us stay connected and help bridge the gap between us. And like any good mother, I always want to know what's going on with my child.

In 2010, Debbie and her family lived in an exclusive area of Virginia near the Virginia State University campus. She'd been renting a lovely brick home there that they loved, but she'd been having a series of conflicts with her landlord. During one of our phone conversations toward the end of 2010, she was crying on the phone as she described their latest dispute.

"Debbie, stop crying!" I told her. "I'll buy a house for you and your family." "Oh my goodness, Mommy—are you serious?" she asked excitedly. "Yes," I responded. She paused, as if in disbelief. "Thank you, Mommy!" she said. She was crying, but she told me she'd ask Anita, her friend at church who sells real estate, if she could show them some homes.

After Debbie hung up, I just sat there, stunned, as I stared at my phone in amazement. What had I done? What had I said? What had I committed myself to? It was another déjà vu moment, reminding me of my reaction when Sister Ashe asked me to speak at the Missionary Annual Day Service Celebration. Just like before, I heard myself say it, but it seemed as the words just rolled out of my mouth as if they were coming from someone else. Even though it has happened to me often, it still catches me by surprise and is always an overwhelming experience. I knew God made me offer to buy Debbie a house, so I knew I had to do it.

After much searching, Debbie's friend Anita was able to find a house for Debbie and her family. I purchased the house for them in November 2011. I committed to pay the down payment and let the house stay in my name until they were better situated to transfer it to theirs; that way, Debbie and Johnell would have the opportunity to see if they could afford the house. They usually paid the mortgage, but when they weren't able to, I was there to support them. The house also needed significant repairs, which I paid for with God's help.

I purchased this home for my daughter Debbie and her family in 2011.

Over the next few years, Debbie and her husband made a diligent effort to pay off their bills and increase their credit score. Six years later, in March 2017, they celebrated their success of making the transfer of the deed from my name to theirs. The house belongs to them now—"lock, stock, and barrel," as the old saying goes—and the two of them and their daughter love their new home. Having an open heart allowed God to speak through me and use me for His purpose. I'm happy He chose to use me as a catalyst to catapult my daughter and her family into home ownership.

Lesson #8: No matter how difficult the task, faith in God removes all obstacles. (2012)

In late fall of 2012, Sister Stedman Ashe, chairperson of the Abyssinian Baptist Church Mission Auxiliary, asked me to represent our church and run as a candidate in the Second Annual Queen Rally.

 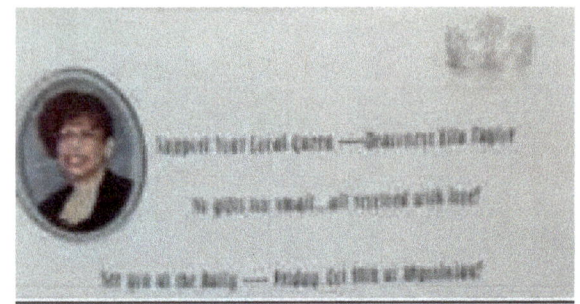

The announcement of my candidacy for the Second Annual Queen Rally.

The Queen Rally was a fundraiser to raise money for high school students who would be starting college the following year. I've always been an advocate for education and have always supported efforts pertaining to educational achievement, so of course I agreed to participate in the rally.

I consider this one of my life lessons because of how difficult it was to raise money and make my campaign work, but I had faith that God wanted me to do it and that He would help me. I created and circulated fund-raising forms, asked family and friends, sent out more than 200 emails, and sent booster sheets to my close friends and relatives to distribute. I did everything I'd been told should be done, yet nothing seemed to bring in substantial funds. The process wasn't working as well as I'd hoped, and my teammates and I were very disappointed.

I was at my wit's end and didn't know what else to try, so I decided to quit. One Sunday morning in the spring of 2013, I resolutely marched myself into Pastor Simmons's office and announced, "Pastor, I'm quitting the contest." Pastor Simmons was very solemn and appeared to be in deep thought, his face expressionless. "Is there a problem?" he asked me. "Yes—many, many problems," I told him. "Nothing is working. No one is interested." I began to give him all the details. He was very supportive, encouraging me not to quit if I was truly serious about wanting to win and contributing to the scholarship fund. He assured me he'd help me, even offering to make announcements during Sunday services in an effort to gain support. Pastor

Simmons kept his word. He announced reminders from the pulpit on a number of occasions and solicited support himself from his constituency in the Newark community.

As our efforts began to pay off, my attitude changed. Pastor Simmons's help really jump-started my campaign and motivated my teammates to think of creative ways to bring in donations. Sister Deadra Gibbons, president of the Women's Auxiliary, contacted me regularly to encourage me and give me advice. My friends and family—especially my daughters—started to solicit donations more proactively. Sister Ida Williams and the Women of Purpose group, led by our late First Lady Emma P. Simmons, spearheaded a number of fundraisers in support of my candidacy, but two of the events—a huge bake sale and a popular book sale—were spectacular and generated a significant amount of money. Church members and friends were strong supporters of all our events, and the money started rolling in. Eventually, the campaign became so successful that I had to open a bank account at Bank of America. I called it "my BOA queen account."

I ultimately won the rally by a landslide, raising thousands of dollars to help graduating high school students afford college.

Representing the Abyssinian Baptist Church, I was thrilled to be crowned the winner of the Second Annual Queen Rally.

Winning the rally was a major hurdle for me. It showed me how powerful God can be when I'm obedient to his voice and remain steadfast in my faith in Him and in myself. The old adage remains true: Winners never quit, and quitters never win.

(left) Deacon James E. Clark walked me down the aisle after I won the Second Annual Queen Rally.
(right) My biography in the program.

Giving my acceptance speech as winner of the Second Annual Queen Rally.

Lesson #9: I must forgive people who are dishonest and lie to get money. (2013)

I'd been driving my 2002 Mercedes for eleven years. I'd given a lot of thought to buying a new car, and of course the area dealerships were also hounding me to buy one, but I felt there was no need to do so because "Baby Gray" was running fine.

At 7 a.m. February 13, as I attempted to make a left turn into the parking lot of the office building where I worked, a line of oncoming cars kindly stopped to let me turn. As I proceeded into the turn, an old red pickup truck came speeding up the shoulder. The vehicle crashed into my left bumper at 45 mph, crushing it on impact and nearly demolishing my car. I realized Baby Gray was about to die, so I immediately turned into the first empty parking spot I saw. Baby Gray took her final breath about two-thirds of the way into the parking spot. Fumes were gushing out from under her hood, and pieces of metal were scattered around the street where the pickup truck had made contact. Red paint laced the face of Baby Gray's hood, and her license plate had been ripped from her bumper and lay crumpled in the middle of the street, blocking traffic.

I called Vanya, my co-worker Michael, and my friend Minnie to come to my rescue. Some bystanders helped us push Baby Gray all the way into the parking space. I called my insurance company, and the campus police arrived and completed the accident report by talking with me and the driver of the pickup truck. He and his vehicle seemed to be totally unharmed, and he drove away.

Vanya was late for work, so Minnie helped me across Bergen Street to University Hospital. I asked Michael to let my director know what had happened and that I was going to the hospital to be checked for injuries.

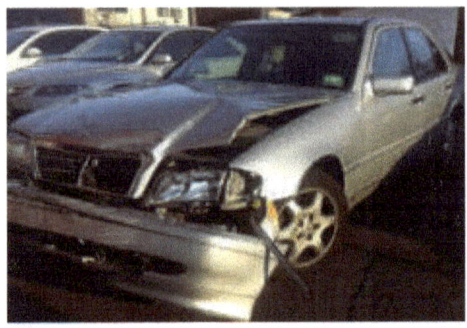 

When my 2002 Mercedes C300, Baby Gray (left), was totaled, I purchased a 2012 Mercedes C300, Sassy Sally, to replace her.

When Minnie and I arrived at the emergency room, the attending aide on duty told us that the driver of the pickup truck had arrived before I did. She also said he was a company employee who was known for rushing because he was always late to work. The driver was being examined by another ER attendant because he'd claimed to be badly hurt. I was also checked for injuries, but I was given clearance to leave when none were found.

A day or two later, my insurance company called me to tell me my car wasn't salvageable and had been towed to their storage yard. I had to pay $500 to use a rental car until I could buy myself another car, which took about six weeks. About a week after the accident, the insurance company notified me that the driver of the pickup truck was suing my insurance company and me for medical and personal damages.

Over the next few months, I had to attend several depositions about the driver's medical claims—the first two with the insurance company adjusters only and the third and last one with the other driver, also. He told his version of what happened, and I told mine. He continued to insist that I was at fault and he was hurt, even though the attendant at the ER had told Minnie and me that he was unharmed. Additionally, a witness to the accident submitted his notarized statement to the insurance company. The statement indicated that I was stopped while the line of oncoming traffic was waiting for me to turn left but that the driver of the red truck had driven up the shoulder at 45 mph, crashing into my vehicle. Although the witness clearly stated I wasn't at fault, the other driver was awarded $16,400. He was a dishonest person who lied to get money from the insurance company.

Lesson #10: God will intervene and force a positive life move. (2013)

The second part of the story about my accident is how I got my new car. This was truly an act of My Best Friend, God. During the first three weeks after the car accident, I went to a number of Mercedes dealerships looking for a car to replace my beloved Baby Gray. I finally found a white Mercedes C300, so I paid a $500 deposit so that I could try it out for a couple of days. I asked my friend and mechanic, Lee, owner of L & J Motors, to check it out for me. Lee found a problem with the car and recommended that the dealership retrieve it from his shop and refund my deposit. The dealership was reluctant to cooperate but finally did pick his car up and return my money. I was thrilled that Lee saved me from buying a car with a problem, and he assured me he'd find me a reliable vehicle. Within a week, Lee called me and directed me to a different Mercedes dealership, where he'd found two cars for me to choose from.

Per a quote by Napoleon Hill, every adversity carries the seed of an equal or greater benefit. In my heart, I know My Best Friend made way for this greater benefit for me. The car I chose is a beautiful, fashionable Mercedes C300 that I named "Sassy Sally." I love her so very much, and I've had no problems with her since I bought her in May 2013. Baby Gray was eleven years old, so I guess God decided I deserved a new one. Sassy Sally has been such a wonderful gift from God and has taken some of the sting out of the anguish and inconvenience I experienced in life lesson #9.

Lesson #11: If I'm afraid to move to the next level of my life, God will move me. (2014)

This was as one of the most difficult life lessons for me to learn. The challenge stemmed from fear—I was afraid to return to my home in Hillsborough, which held all the memories of my life with Willie. I had forced the memories out of my head, keeping them safely tucked away in Hillsborough. Now I know it was a defense mechanism, because I had to protect myself.

I'd been living in that one little room—my safe haven—since my daughter had given up her office for me seven years ago. I'd known for a long time that it was time to return home. My heart said yes. My Best Friend, God, said yes. But my feet—my feet were stuck, and I couldn't make them move toward Hillsborough.

But My Best Friend has a sense of humor. He often appears to play our game, but in reality, He is always working His own plan for our higher good. That's what happened when He used my nephew, Roger Brown, as His instrument to get me unstuck. In the fall of 2013, Roger asked me if he could move into my Hillsborough home. I was surprised at his request, but I agreed. Roger is a responsible, hardworking young adult, and I was honored to know he would be on site to keep things in order for me.

Roger shared many stories with me about his time in Hillsborough, but to me, the funniest one was about his war with the mice. Because the house was otherwise uninhabited, some mice felt entitled to take up residence there and have a hearty daily party. But Roger would have none of it. Not only did he set mousetraps and poison to catch or kill them, but he often set himself up as the night watchman to take an active role in their demise. Roger had decided he didn't want rodents as roommates, so they had to go.

Roger had been living at my home for about a year when I made the big leap of faith. In June 2014, I woke up one morning and vowed to My Best Friend that I'd move back to my home on my birthday later that month. I didn't hear, feel, or sense any opposition, so I packed up all my belongings to add to my existing massive accumulation of stuff in Hillsborough.

Seven years after I'd moved in, I returned home on my birthday as planned, feeling very proud of myself for keeping my commitment to myself and to My Best Friend. I believe the seven-year period was a completion for me. I've read that the number *seven* is significant. Scholars say it's the number of perfection and of God's completion. God created the world in seven days; the word *created* is used seven times in the Bible to describe God's creative work; there are seven days in a week, and the Holy Sabbath was originally the seventh day; and the Bible was originally divided into seven sections. Also, I lost Willie in 2007 and lived at my daughter's home for seven years. This suggests a connection to the number seven. I believe the significance is a seven-year completion period for me, starting a new physical and spiritual cycle.

As much as I wanted to be back in my home, it was very difficult for me to analyze, understand, and solve the many issues facing me when I returned. But I had the support of My Best Friend, who helped me adjust and gave me guidance in approaching such a humongous task. Roger continued to live with me for five months, until he needed to move closer to his place of work. But as we all know, there is a reason and a season for everything. My nephew had completed the task God charged him to do.

There are two reasons I'll always remember Roger's time at my home with gratitude. First, I believe he was obedient to God's direction to come to my rescue even though I didn't know I was being rescued. Having Roger live in my home eventually made it easier for me to move back home; otherwise, I might not have gone back at all. Second, during the time he was living in my home, there was a powerful storm that almost completely destroyed my beloved Okame Cherry tree. Roger repaired the damage from the storm, bandaging the tree and nursing her back to health over a number of weeks. So now, whenever I look at that tree, I think of Roger, his kind heart, and everything he did to help his Auntie Ella.

I realize now that My Best Friend orchestrated this entire event. It relates to my path and to my new life. Having a directed path is the subject of a frequently quoted and a very well loved Bible verse about life: *Trust in the Lord with all your heart, and lean not on your own understanding. In all your ways acknowledge Him, and He shall direct your paths.* (Proverbs 3:5-6) It took me a long time to fully appreciate the value of God's direction. I know that trusting in God, even when things don't make sense, is the key to my life. During those seven years when I couldn't see my path, I could only see to the next bend in the road—I couldn't see around it. But My Best Friend could see around the corner, and He still can and does.

Lesson #12: In a complicated situation, I must listen for God's guidance. (2015)

When I moved back into my home in Hillsborough in June 2014, I was both happy and sad—happy because my home is where my heart is and sad because everything was out of order there. Everywhere I looked, there was something to be repaired, moved, replaced, or discarded. The disarray put me in somewhat of a tailspin, because I'm a very organized person. The Holy Spirit spoke to my heart and directed me to make a prioritized list of everything that needed to be done. Taking time to focus on my prioritized list created some calmness in me that began to influence my thoughts and behavior, and I started to feel happy again.

I had enjoyed having my nephew Roger live in my home to talk with me, share meals with me, and keep me company. So when he moved out in late November 2014 to shorten his commute to work, I felt lonely and realized I had some repressed feelings about living by myself. My situation seemed somewhat complicated.

But lo and behold, My Best Friend had a plan for me—a plan to place my new "daughter by another mother," Kymberly Evelyn, in my path. She and her family moved into my home during the summer of 2015, but it took some time before I realized how significant she would become in my life.

Even though my new living situation appeared to be by happenstance, I knew in my heart that it was God's plan. He was watching me in my challenging position, and I was listening for his guidance. And just like many other times in my life, a situation that originally seemed to be negative turned out to be a positive change thanks to God's love for me.

This plan for me had been set in motion a few years earlier by a storm that flooded my basement and destroyed about 75 percent of its contents. So I asked Troy, my contractor and right-hand man for all my repair work, to address the next item on my prioritized list: basement repair. It was a humungous task, because so many things had to be thrown away and the entire basement area had to be cleared out before repairs could even begin. We started the project in the spring of 2015.

A few months later, the basement was in great shape. In fact, it looked so good that I felt it was beautiful enough for someone to live in and enjoy. I had a sudden and striking realization—an epiphany—to contact Home Sharing, the organization Willie used to volunteer with, to see if any of their clients were in need of a place to live. That's how God introduced Kym into my life. She moved into my home with her two daughters on July 23, 2015, and has been living there ever since. Kym has become my third daughter, and I love her dearly. I believe it was God's plan all along for her to move into my home so we could bond and share love and friendship.

Lesson #13: In times of indecision, if I stay still, God will provide a solution. (2017)

Willie and I had planned to retire in 2012 and travel the world. We wanted to return to Hawaii and Paris, and we planned to go to Africa and some other places we hadn't been. But his untimely death put my retirement plans in a tailspin, so I was very indecisive. It's a common behavior among humans—sometimes, when we don't know what to do, we do nothing. Besides having lost my incentive to retire, I wasn't even sure I could afford to. So I didn't act. But My Best Friend provided a solution.

I continued working, but a few years after Willie's death, I finally decided to be proactive and assess my financial situation. With the help of some financial experts, I reviewed my pension fund, mutual fund, IRA, annuities, life insurance policy, and emergency funds. All the professionals gave me similar feedback: from a financial perspective, I was in a position to retire whenever I was ready.

Even so, I was hesitant because I didn't know what I would do with myself. So I simply kept working. My Best Friend continued to give me signs telling me I could retire, but I couldn't see them clearly because I was paralyzed with fear. I had worked all my life, so I was uncomfortable living without having a paycheck coming in.

My Best Friend was watching me, and He sent me two clear indications that I should retire. First, in the fall of 2016, Rutgers University offered the services of professionals from their designated wealth-management firm to evaluate my financial portfolio, as they did for all of their employees near retirement age. It was nine years after Willie's death and four years after my planned retirement. The financial experts gave me a formal report of the results of their study, in which they calculated that I had enough money to last me until I was at least 100 years old based on my current spending. I was very pleased with the report, but I still didn't retire. I was stuck.

So, My Best Friend provided me with a second blatant indicator. On May 17, 2017, my newly hired executive director and my director informed me that our department was being reorganized. I was laid off from my position as a database administrator, and that day was my last official day of work there.

The benefits department informed me that my options were to either retire or find another position at the university within a year.

I enjoyed the time I was laid off so much that I decided to retire before my one-year deadline. My eyes were finally open, and I could see that My Best Friend had provided me an entire year to see around the corner and to realize that I needed to have more faith in Him. I was able to see that I was indeed financially secure, and that I had plenty of things to do to keep myself busy and enough money to do them.

One of the best things I did after I retired was to join Planet Fitness gym in August 2017. In two years, I lost 20 pounds, became stronger and fitter, and made many new friends. To this day, these friends continue to provide a significant social outlet for me. We have a lot of fun together during our training classes, and sometimes we socialize outside of the gym. We refer to one another as "gym buddies," but we're more like family because we have a special kind of love for each other.

Me (center) with my Planet Fitness gym buddies: (back row left to right) Geraldine, Stan, Doug, and Sandy. (front row, left to right) Annette, Gail, Ella, and Liz. Not pictured: Patti, Paul, Yvette, Cathy, Debi, Liza, Christine, Francine, Agnes, Ellen, and Mary Jane.

I continue to keep the Prayer of Jabez in my heart and on my lips, and My Best Friend continues to answer my prayer. For 30 years, I've been using that scripture as a guide for my life. *(And Jabez called on the God of Israel saying, "Oh, that You would bless me indeed, and enlarge my territory, that Your hand would be with me, and that You would keep me from evil, that I may not cause pain!" So God granted him what he requested.* [1 Chronicles 4:10]) God continues to enlarge my territory, and I continue to exercise the joy of giving. I retired six years later than I'd planned, but God managed the process much better than I ever could have. In retirement, I still exercise that important lesson I learned from my mother, Margaret Estelle Branch: "Save a little for a rainy day."

Lesson #14: God facilitates His plan for my life. (2018)

Sometime around 2014, I started to feel a burning desire to tell the world about my life. The desire was so strong that I was sure God had put it in my spirit, and I realized that writing a book was an important component of His plan for my life. I felt I had to let the world know that God loves each and every one of his children equally, per His word. *(Then Peter opened his mouth and said: "In truth I perceive that God shows no partiality." [Acts 10:34])* He will show Himself to us and guide us on our journey through life as we establish an intimate relationship with Him and remain obedient to His voice, His guidance, and His word. *(If you love Me, keep My commandments. [John 14:15])*

I began to see clearly that with all I had accomplished in my life, I couldn't possibly have done it without My Best Friend, God. I needed to share with the world that I felt as if I'd been taken by my hand and walked through my life as if I had a spiritual guide walking in front of me. In many cases, I felt as if I'd walked over burning-hot coals of fire and didn't even feel them. My Best Friend was always there for me and with me.

I had set a mental date for after the holidays were over in 2017 to start writing my book, but I came up with a variety of excuses not to. My most palatable excuse was that I didn't have a place to write. I'd had an office in my home for many years, but it had become very cluttered and disorganized in the seven years since I'd lost my husband and moved in with my daughter. So, I decided to set up a new office for myself. Over the years, I had removed most of the furnishings, wall decorations, and other decor from Willie's office where he used to run his tax and accounting business. I had donated all the usable items to the Vietnam Veterans of America, the Lupus Foundation of America, and the Salvation Army. Willie's office was larger than mine, so I decided to renovate it, make it my own, and create a beautiful new place to write my book. So once again, in January of 2018, I called on my contractor, Troy. Troy was the perfect choice because he'd worked on my house many times before. He was familiar with the structure of my house. He had previously worked on important essentials like electrical and plumbing, was dependable, always made himself available for my projects, and charged a fair price. Troy completed my new office in about two months.

My next challenge was to decorate my new office to my liking. I felt the most important item was my desk. I knew exactly what I wanted, but it wasn't easy to find for a reasonable price. I searched online and at a number of high-quality furniture stores, but to no avail. After about six months, I found exactly what I wanted at Ashley Homestore for a very reasonable sale price of $1,650, including a beautiful, comfortable chair. The icing on the cake: I had twelve months to finance with zero interest.

I was thrilled with my new desk, but there was still a lot to do. I had a visual image of how I wanted my office to look. I knew my theme would be blue, and I needed some other things. I wanted to find a specific style blue chaise lounge for my corner reading and a blue feathered 5'x7' throw rug. Then I'd need to decorate my walls and find the perfect place for other accents, including my favorite blue painting.

The color blue has always been very special to me because it's the color of the sea and the sky, and looking at the sea and the sky has always brought me a sense of peace and made me feel connected to my Creator. From a spiritual perspective, blue is associated with truth, tranquility, and creativity and is thought to symbolize heaven. So I felt using blue was a good way to bring added value to the surroundings I needed to enhance my writing.

I had a difficult time finding the right chaise, rug, swag curtains, and vertical blinds because I needed to see them to make sure they were what I wanted. With all the time and effort I was putting into decorating my office, I was becoming somewhat exasperated. After about four months, and only with God's help, I finally found everything I wanted.

I felt I wasn't able to write my book until I had the tranquil space in which to do it. My new office turned out even more amazing than I had visualized, and it's just what I wanted because God orchestrated the plan for it. In fact, I tell people that I feel in my spirit that God decorated it. Here are some pictures of the beautiful office He helped me create so I could write my story.

My new office furniture

My new swag curtains and vertical blinds.

(left) My new blue chaise lounge in my reading corner.

(right) The view of my office from the entrance.

Lesson #15: God sends help in unexpected ways. (2018)

It took nearly a year—from January 2018 until November 2018—to renovate my new office space where I was to write my book. That's when God intervened to connect me with someone who would offer me a tool to help me write my book. This is how it came about.

One of the many significant acquaintances I made at a Planet Fitness training class was a young woman named Kym. One day we started chatting, and Kym mentioned that she was an instructor for a class called "How to Make a Book." I was astonished, but at the same time I was delighted to hear about it. She invited me to attend her class, and I jumped at the chance. It turned out to be a marvelous class for seniors, with about fifteen students; Kym and another teacher, Mike; and the class editor, Jackie. I started attending the class in November 2018, which was the same month I completed my office. God sent me help in an unexpected way to propel me to write my book at the appropriate time.

It was a divine appointment, and it reminded me that God knows the right time to meet every single need we have. Sometimes he waits a long time and we give up, but if we are patient and persistent, we can relax knowing God will fulfill His promises. If we ask or even just desire something that is within God's plan for our lives, it will be fulfilled. I believe my experience demonstrates that an intimate relationship with our Lord will make our life's journey live up to our potential. Throughout the years, I have seen God's greatness, His love, and His blessings in such awesome ways, and it has shown me the power of knowing Him and making sure that He is first in my life and that I maintain an intimate relationship with Him.

My Angels

I've come to realize that since the death of my husband Willie, angels have been an important influence in my life. They are my *earth angels*—not the heavenly angels mentioned in the Bible, like Michael and Gabriel, but human angels that God has strategically placed in my path. Each of them serves a specific purpose, performing a function that helps make my life work with little effort on my part. These people have been sent to me by God to help me fulfill His plan for my life.

Before I share the names of my earth angels and the role of each one in my life, I'd like to explain more about earth angels, based on information from the website Learning Mind (https://www.learning-mind.com/earth-angel/). My hope is that my experience and research will help you recognize your own earth angels so that you may be open to accepting the gifts they can offer you.

What Is an Earth Angel?

Unlike heavenly angels, earth angels are human beings. Many of them feel they've been sent to earth for a higher purpose. In fact, one of my earth angels actually told me she's here to make life better for other people.

Earth angels also share some characteristics that might not be obvious. For example, I continue to be amazed at how two of my earth angels know how to repair absolutely anything. Electric lamps, vacuum cleaners, plumbing—you name it, they can fix it. Below are some other traits that earth angels tend to have:

- Many earth angels have some kind of artistic talent, like drawing, singing, or writing. Several of my earth angels are good singers, and one writes beautiful poetry.

- Some become overwhelmed in large groups of people. That's because there may be an abundance of energy where many people are present. I've noticed that one of my earth angels will go off into a corner by herself when she's in a large group of people.

- Some of my earth angels look very young for their age, which is another common characteristic of earth angels.

- Earth angels often have an energy that people are naturally drawn to. I experienced this with many of my angels when I met them. I once took one of them to church with me, and at least ten people later told me they liked her and wanted to know when she'd be going back. She even exchanged contact information with one of the church members.

- They may be irresponsible or have trouble managing their time, because they're often helping others instead. This is true of at least one of my earth angels, who just can't seem to be on time for most things.

- Earth angels are usually independent. They rarely ask for help, because they feel it's their duty to help others. In one instance, I offered to help one of my angels buy a new vehicle because his was on its last legs. He agreed at first, but he later figured out a way not to let me help him.

• They often openly ask for reassurance from the significant people in their lives. That stems from their tendency to be very honest—a trait I've noticed in some of my own earth angels.

• Most earth angels are open-minded and accepting rather than being judgmental. Recently, in a conversation with one of my earth angels, he mentioned the scripture reflecting that concept: *Judge not, that you be not judged.* (Matthew 7:1)

• Generally, earth angels are highly in tune with nature. They feel most comfortable outdoors; it energizes them. One of my earth angels tells me she must have some type of daily commune with nature. She says it revitalizes her and clears her mind.

• Earth angels typically have a very powerful sense of intuition, exhibiting sound judgment and keen perception. A few of my angels tend to analyze situations—sometimes for themselves and sometimes for me.

• Although they enjoy helping people, they cherish time they spend in solitude, which allows them to recharge their healing energies. One of my earth angels, when he's going through a hard time, tends to basically go into hiding until his situation has improved. I've often asked him afterward why he didn't call me so we could work it out together. His usual response: "I just needed to be by myself for a while."

• Many earth angels are empaths: they feel what other people feel. They hate to see others in pain, but they also feel others' joy. I've seen these traits in some of my earth angels.

• Earth angels are generally non-confrontational, opting for peaceful resolutions to conflict. For example: one of my earth angels will find an excuse to end our telephone conversation if negative subjects or disagreements arise.

These are common characteristics of earth angels that I've also noticed in my own angels. If you pay attention to the actions of those close to you and are open to the possibility that you may have earth angels of your own, you might be able to identify them. And if such a phenomenon does exist in your life, you may wish to express gratitude to your Creator.

Listed below are my earth angels, along with the function each one serves in making my life work. (Note: You'll notice I don't use my earth angels' last names, because they'll know who they are when they read this.)

Name	Function
1. Stan	Financial Advisor/Friend
2. Troy	Property Caretaker/Renovator/Helper/Friend
3. Jack	Investment Advisor/Financial Consultant
4. Mark	Investment Advisor/Financial Consultant
5. Harry	Investment Advisor/Financial Consultant
6. Vanya	Business Assistant/Analyzer/Confidant
7. Deborah	Researcher/Liaison/Confidant
8. Kym	Tenant/Friend/Sounding Board/Event Planner
9. Roger	Property Caretaker
10. Cheryl	Friend/Spiritual Advisor/Confidant
11. Herby	Artist/Helper/Godson/Friend
12. Howard	Lawyer/Legal Advisor
13. Juan	Landscaper
14. Kim	Friend/Helper/"Plus One" at Social Events
15. Wallace	Devoted Brother
16. Marcelle	Graphic Designer/Friend

My Five Tips for Living a Better Life

Tip #1: Pay attention to your intuition.

Our intuition is the inner voice of our soul. Intuition is like a muscle: the more we work it, the stronger it gets. Most of us use our intuition on a daily basis and don't even realize it. Everyone has intuition. Intuition is an instinctive feeling; it doesn't require conscious reasoning.

Tip #2: Welcome divine guidance into your life.

To do this, all you have to do is ask God and then stay open to the signs He offers to you. Communicating with God through Jesus Christ and the Holy Spirit can be an effective way to enhance your intuition, because often, if you're open enough, you will receive signs to help validate your intuitive hunches.

Tip #3: Do things to help you be fruitful for the rest of your life. (Inspired by Charles Stanley: https://www.youtube.com/watch?v=_qz5ya4D_nQ)

- ✓ Keep learning:

  It's good for you!

  A lazy brain ages more quickly.

  Sudoku has been a daily tool for me for many, many years. You may wish to find a tool to stimulate your brain.

- ✓ Keep loving:

  It's an important part of staying young.

  It promotes good health.

  It raises self-esteem.

- ✓ Keep laughing:

  Laughing has many positive effects on health. It releases some of the body's natural chemicals that relieve stress, reduce pain, and boost the immune system.

  Negative emotions like sadness and stress can cause chronic pain, sleep problems, and many other health issues.

- ✓ Keep leaving:

  Leave your cares behind instead of dragging them into your present.

Put your anxiety on God's shoulders and He will help you carry it.

> *Casting all your care upon Him, for He cares for you.* (1 Peter 5:7)

✓ Keep dreaming:

Put your future in God's hands.

> I feel young, youthful, and useful at such a seasoned age, and I'll stay this way for as long as I keep planning for tomorrow.

Don't ever quit—because quitters never win and winners never quit.

✓ Keep looking:

Look your best.

> I'm always very meticulous about how I look.

Do your best.

> I always strive for the A.

Be your best.

> I always give 100 percent to everything I do.

✓ Keep laboring:

Don't ever stop being fruitful.

> *I am the vine, you are the branches. He who abides in Me, and I in him, bears much fruit; for without Me you can do nothing.* (John 15:5)

Stay involved in activities; make yourself useful.

Have faith in God and confidence in yourself.

Every time you do something, do it better than you did it the last time.

✓ Keep leaning:

Lean on and depend on our Lord Jesus Christ.

Trust God and acknowledge Him.

> *Trust in the Lord with all your heart; and lean not unto your own understanding. In all your ways acknowledge Him, and He shall direct your paths.* (Proverbs 3:5-6)

✓ Keep listening:

Listen to God.

God speaks to us in many ways; learn how to discern His voice.

When you need guidance, ask God to speak to your heart.

Follow the guidance God gives you; His direction will help you be righteous and allow you to continue to be fruitful.

> *The righteous shall flourish like a palm tree; he shall grow like a cedar in Lebanon. Those who are planted in the house of the Lord shall flourish in the courts of our God. They shall still bear fruit in old age; they shall be fresh and flourishing.* (Psalm 92:12-14)

I desire to do these things daily so I can continue to be fruitful. I want each and every day of my life to count. I want to be useful all the days of my life.

What about you—would you like to be fruitful for the rest of your life? If you do, just ask God for guidance and He will show you how.

Tip #4: There are eight habits of a godly life.

1. Pray.

> *Be anxious for nothing, but in everything by prayer and supplication, with thanksgiving, let your requests be made known to God.* (Philippians 4:6)

2. Trust in God and have faith in Him.

> *Have I not commanded you? Be strong and of good courage; do not be afraid, nor be dismayed, for the Lord your God is with you wherever you go.* (Joshua 1:9)

3. Meditate on God's word.

> *But his delight is in the law of the Lord, and in His law he meditates day and night.* (Psalm 1:2)

4. Obey God.

> *Now therefore, if you will indeed obey My voice and keep My covenant, then you shall be a special treasure to Me above all people; for all the earth is Mine.* (Exodus 19:5)

5. Surrender your life to the indwelling Holy Spirit.

> *Do you not know that you are the temple of God and that the Spirit of God dwells in you?* (1 Corinthians 3:16)

6. Forgive others.

> *For if you forgive men their trespasses, your heavenly Father will also forgive you. But if you do not forgive men their trespasses, neither will your Father forgive your trespasses.* (Matthew 6:14-15)

7. Give to God. My reference here is to give your tithe and offerings. I understand this concept, and I believe 100 percent in this scripture, so I'm diligent in my tithing and offerings.

> *Will a man rob God? Yet you have robbed Me! But you say, "In what way have we robbed You?" In tithes and offerings. You are cursed with a curse, for you have robbed Me, even this whole nation. Bring all the tithes into the storehouse, that there may be food in My house, and try Me now in this, if I will not open for you the windows of heaven and pour out for you such blessing that there will not be room enough to receive it.* (Malachi 3:8-10)

8. Give to others.

> *Now this I say, he who sows sparingly will also reap sparingly, and he who sows bountifully will also reap bountifully. Each one must do just as he has purposed in his heart, not grudgingly or under compulsion, for God loves a cheerful giver. And God is able to make all grace abound to you, so that always having all sufficiency in everything, you may have abundance for every good deed.* (2 Corinthians 9:6-8)

Tip #5: Treasure your true friends; they are gifts from God.

A true friend:

- Loves you as you are
- Sees not only who you are now, but who you can become
- Is there to catch you when you fall
- Is someone you can share your everyday experiences with
- Accepts you at your worst, but helps you become your best
- Understands your past, and believes in your future
- Accepts you unconditionally, just the way you are—both the positive characteristics and the negative ones
- Stands by your side when everyone else has left you

Putting It All Together

Now I Know that my life is on purpose—God's purpose.

Now I Know that life as I experience it may appear haphazard and unpredictable, but God has His plan for my life.

Now I Know that since God created me with free will, I must fit into His plan by having an intimate relationship with Him, trusting Him, listening to His voice, and being obedient to His direction.

In my earlier years, I didn't know why I was always so fanatical about self-improvement. This book is about self-improvement. I've been a student of self-improvement for as long as I can remember—always studying: using books and tapes like *Life and Teaching of the Masters of the Far East, A Course in Miracles, Pathways to Mastership, It's Time for You, The Secret, The Purpose Driven Life*, and others. Over the years, I've also regularly practiced meditation and yoga and used other self-development tools.

I was inspired by God to tell my story. He orchestrated all the details: from setting up my office so I could write it; to sending Kym to Planet Fitness to meet me and enroll me in her class; to sending Jackie to plunge in and help me get my book on the right track; and even further, to connect me with Dina, the best editor this side of heaven, to guide me through the editorial process…and on and on it continues.

I'm very grateful for the intimate relationship God allows me to have with Him in this regard. I truly believe that God directs my life and that He wanted me to share my story so that it may encourage others by showing my life as a testimony to the world. To show my readers how they, too, can overcome grief and grow themselves. To show them that by establishing *true* intimacy with God, they can overcome anything life throws in their path.

Through my growth process, I have learned:

- To depend on myself from within my spirit

- To hear and depend on God through the connection of my spirit to the Holy Spirit

- That through my obedience to God's guidance, He is molding me into the person He created me to be

- That God continues to grow me into my full potential and His plan for my life

Now I Know that all things come to me not by chance, but on purpose by God's fatherly hand.

Now I Know that with God and through Him, each of us can grow into our full potential and be a disciple of His son Jesus by believing in Jesus and following His example in our daily lives.

Now I Know a better way to live.

My hope is that you'll feel encouraged and empowered by reading my story and that perhaps you've found something in my story that will help you in your life's journey.

About the Author

Ella W. Taylor was born in Chesterfield County, Virginia, to the late Earl and Margaret Branch. She is one of seven children, with three sisters and three brothers. She was raised in a Christian home, and at the young age of 13, she accepted Christ, got baptized, and became a member of the Union Grove Baptist Church. In 1986, she joined the Abyssinian Baptist Church in Newark, New Jersey, and is still a member there today.

Ella lives in Hillsborough, New Jersey. She has been a widow since 2007, when her beloved husband, Deacon Willie R. Taylor, was murdered. She has two daughters, two sons-in-law, five grandchildren, and two great-grandchildren. Her family and friends regard her as a devoted and loving mother, mother-in-law, grandmother, aunt, sister, and friend. She is appreciated for being the rescuer when it comes to providing a helping hand and is admired for her kindness and thoughtfulness toward others.

Ella attended high school in Virginia before relocating to New Jersey in 1968. She received a bachelor's degree in management science from Kean University, Union, New Jersey, in 1979; a bachelor's degree in computer science from Kean University in 1983; and an MBA in managerial finance from Pace University, New York, in 1987.

Ella has a solid background in computer science and higher education management. For ten years, she worked for AT&T Bell Laboratories, where she started as a computer programmer and later became a head of the text-processing department. She was a professor at Essex County College, Newark, for nine years, teaching courses in computer information science. She worked for Rutgers University, Newark, as a database developer and website designer. She later served as the database administrator of the Office of Faculty Affairs until she retired in 2018 after twenty-two years with the university.

Ella believes the body is a precious vessel on loan to us by God and that it should be handled with care and respect. For that reason, she is a strong advocate for cleanliness, physical appearance, physical exercise, and modest food intake.

Ella has an intimate relationship with the Lord. She believes that education and knowledge are powerful tools and that the beginning of true knowledge starts with a very personal relationship with Jesus Christ. She is a learned scholar who enjoys bearing witness to others about Christ and sharing her wisdom about how to live a life of purpose, driven by core beliefs and values. Her favorite song is "Never Could Have Made It," by Marvin Sapp. Her favorite scripture is Mark 11:24: *Therefore I say to you, whatever things you ask when you pray, believe that you receive them, and you will have them.*